Sports and
Athletes

OPPOSING VIEWPOINTS®

OTHER BOOKS OF RELATED INTEREST

Sports and Athletes

OPPOSING VIEWPOINTS®

Laura K. Egendorf, Book Editor

David L. Bender, *Publisher*
Bruno Leone, *Executive Editor*
Bonnie Szumski, *Editorial Director*
David Haugen, *Managing Editor*

OPPOSING
VIEWPOINTS®
SERIES

Greenhaven Press, Inc., San Diego, California

Cover photo: Branbtner and Staedler

Library of Congress Cataloging-in-Publication Data

Sports and athletes : opposing viewpoints / Laura K. Egendorf, book
    editor.
        p.   cm. — (Opposing viewpoints series)
    Includes bibliographical references and index.
    ISBN 0-7377-0057-2 (lib. : alk. paper). —
ISBN 0-7377-0056-4 (pbk. : alk. paper)
    1. Sports—Moral and ethical aspects. 2. Sports—Social aspects.
I. Egendorf, Laura K., 1973–   . II. Series: Opposing viewpoints series
(Unnumbered)
GV706.3.S668 1999
796—dc21   98-32022
                                                                CIP

Greenhaven Press, Inc., P.O. Box 289009
San Diego, CA 92198-9009

"CONGRESS SHALL MAKE NO LAW...ABRIDGING THE FREEDOM OF SPEECH, OR OF THE PRESS."

First Amendment to the U.S. Constitution

The basic foundation of our democracy is the First Amendment guarantee of freedom of expression. The Opposing Viewpoints Series is dedicated to the concept of this basic freedom and the idea that it is more important to practice it than to enshrine it.

CONTENTS

WHY CONSIDER OPPOSING VIEWPOINTS?

> "The only way in which a human being can make some approach to knowing the whole of a subject is by hearing what can be said about it by persons of every variety of opinion and studying all modes in which it can be looked at by every character of mind. No wise man ever acquired his wisdom in any mode but this."
>
> ### John Stuart Mill

In our media-intensive culture it is not difficult to find differing opinions. Thousands of newspapers and magazines and dozens of radio and television talk shows resound with differing points of view. The difficulty lies in deciding which opinion to agree with and which "experts" seem the most credible. The more inundated we become with differing opinions and claims, the more essential it is to hone critical reading and thinking skills to evaluate these ideas. Opposing Viewpoints books address this problem directly by presenting stimulating debates that can be used to enhance and teach these skills. The varied opinions contained in each book examine many different aspects of a single issue. While examining these conveniently edited opposing views, readers can develop critical thinking skills such as the ability to compare and contrast authors' credibility, facts, argumentation styles, use of persuasive techniques, and other stylistic tools. In short, the Opposing Viewpoints Series is an ideal way to attain the higher-level thinking and reading skills so essential in a culture of diverse and contradictory opinions.

In addition to providing a tool for critical thinking, Opposing Viewpoints books challenge readers to question their own strongly held opinions and assumptions. Most people form their opinions on the basis of upbringing, peer pressure, and personal, cultural, or professional bias. By reading carefully balanced opposing views, readers must directly confront new ideas as well as the opinions of those with whom they disagree. This is not to simplistically argue that everyone who reads opposing views will—or should—change his or her opinion. Instead, the series enhances readers' understanding of their own views by encouraging confrontation with opposing ideas. Careful examination of others' views can lead to the readers' understanding of the logical inconsistencies in their own opinions, perspective on why they hold an opinion, and the consideration of the possibility that their opinion requires further evaluation.

EVALUATING OTHER OPINIONS

To ensure that this type of examination occurs, Opposing Viewpoints books present all types of opinions. Prominent spokespeople on different sides of each issue as well as well-known professionals from many disciplines challenge the reader. An additional goal of the series is to provide a forum for other, less known, or even unpopular viewpoints. The opinion of an ordinary person who has had to make the decision to cut off life support from a terminally ill relative, for example, may be just as valuable and provide just as much insight as a medical ethicist's professional opinion. The editors have two additional purposes in including these less known views. One, the editors encourage readers to respect others' opinions—even when not enhanced by professional credibility. It is only by reading or listening to and objectively evaluating others' ideas that one can determine whether they are worthy of consideration. Two, the inclusion of such viewpoints encourages the important critical thinking skill of objectively evaluating an author's credentials and bias. This evaluation will illuminate an author's reasons for taking a particular stance on an issue and will aid in readers' evaluation of the author's ideas.

As series editors of the Opposing Viewpoints Series, it is our hope that these books will give readers a deeper understanding of the issues debated and an appreciation of the complexity of even seemingly simple issues when good and honest people disagree. This awareness is particularly important in a democratic society such as ours in which people enter into public debate to determine the common good. Those with whom one disagrees should not be regarded as enemies but rather as people whose views deserve careful examination and may shed light on one's own.

Thomas Jefferson once said that "difference of opinion leads to inquiry, and inquiry to truth." Jefferson, a broadly educated man, argued that "if a nation expects to be ignorant and free . . . it expects what never was and never will be." As individuals and as a nation, it is imperative that we consider the opinions of others and examine them with skill and discernment. The Opposing Viewpoints Series is intended to help readers achieve this goal.

David L. Bender & Bruno Leone,
Series Editors

Greenhaven Press anthologies primarily consist of previously published material taken from a variety of sources, including periodicals, books, scholarly journals, newspapers, government documents, and position papers from private and public organizations. These original sources are often edited for length and to ensure their accessibility for a young adult audience. The anthology editors also change the original titles of these works in order to clearly present the main thesis of each viewpoint and to explicitly indicate the opinion presented in the viewpoint. These alterations are made in consideration of both the reading and comprehension levels of a young adult audience. Every effort is made to ensure that Greenhaven Press accurately reflects the original intent of the authors included in this anthology.

INTRODUCTION

"By providing . . . examples of the spirit to win and excel, sport makes a real contribution to our world."
—David Holmquist, Biola University basketball coach

"Perhaps sports were never anything more than a dreamland for the fan."
—Robert Lipsyte, New York Times columnist

Every January, jokes are made about the Super Bowl becoming an unofficial national holiday. Over 133 million Americans watched the 1998 Super Bowl broadcast, providing an example of the popularity of sports in today's world. Millions of people are not just sports fans but participants as well, including 35 million Americans between the ages of six and twenty-one. Although most of these athletes will never gain much recognition or wealth for their efforts, some are among the richest and most famous people in society. Sports have an important place in society, but the question remains as to whether sports and athletes can live up to the expectations that are sometimes placed on them.

Many people believe that participation in sports can build character and teach values such as teamwork and perseverance. This view has its antecedent in the culture of ancient Greece. Katherine Kersten, chair of the Center of the American Experiment, a conservative public policy institution, writes, "The Greeks viewed superiority in running or wrestling as an outward sign of inward nobility of character. Sport, for them, was a metaphor for right conduct in all competitions of life." Today sports are still considered to be an avenue toward self-improvement, but they also function for many youths as an alternative to involvement with drugs or gangs.

At times, sports do live up to high expectations. When baseball player Cal Ripken ended his consecutive-game streak toward the end of the 1998 season, many sportswriters praised Ripken and the work ethic that had helped keep him in the Baltimore Oriole lineup for more than sixteen years. Other athletes are lauded for their charity work or for triumphing over troubled childhoods.

Sports are also praised for what they do for their fans. Sports can bring people together. The Green Bay Packers are considered by many to be an ideal example of how sports can unite a community, because the Packers are the only team in the National Football League (NFL) that is community-owned, rather than in the hands of a wealthy owner who could move the team on a whim. Spectators of all races and social classes are able to unite to cheer for their favorite team. David Holmquist, the men's basketball coach at Biola University in California, writes, "There is something enormously healthy about living in a world of clear and absolute allegiances—at least during a two-hour game. No one has to interpret for rooted fans or players what they are feeling. . . . We are consumed with a singular intention, and that is for our team to do well."

In a perfect world, sports would live up to these and other expectations. But not surprisingly, many athletes, fans, and teams not only fall short of those ideals but also behave in ways that can be especially troubling. For example, some critics assert that too great an emphasis is placed on winning—participation in sports is not seen as the goal, but rather, doing better than everyone else is what matters. This emphasis can manifest itself in parents and coaches who push young athletes too hard, or athletes who use performance-enhancing drugs, or coaches who encourage their athletes to play dirty. D. Stanley Eitzen, a professor emeritus at Colorado State University and prominent sports sociologist, observes, "Sport has a dark side. It is plagued with problems. . . . In the view of many, these problems result from bad people. I believe that stems from a morally distorted sports world—a world where winning supersedes all other considerations."

To some of these observers, sports are not always the best way for children to improve their character or better their lot in life. This issue is of significant interest to people who are concerned with the future of minority children and worry that some of these youngsters place too great an emphasis on sports as a professional career, disregarding other paths to success.

While some athletes are lauded for their behavior, such as Ripken and the late tennis champion Arthur Ashe, the sports pages of America's newspapers provide numerous examples of men and women whose athletic talent is overshadowed by reckless, and sometimes criminal, actions. Stories about an athlete arrested for drug possession or spousal abuse seem to be published nearly every day. Athletes are also criticized for their greed—demands to receive higher salaries or be traded to a team that will pay them what they seek. *San Diego Union-Tribune* columnist Joseph Perkins is among those who believe that athletes should behave more ideally. "Whether they like it or not, whether they asked for it or not, pro athletes are very much public citizens. The American people have a right to expect them to behave themselves in a socially responsible manner."

The behavior of fans often also fails to live up to Holmquist's praise. Racial epithets have been hurled during games. The World Cup has been the site of boorish behavior by soccer hooligans. Even success can bring out the worst in fans, such as riots after a team has won a championship. Eitzen is among those who criticize the more unruly fans when he comments, "Spectator behavior such as rioting and throwing objects at players and officials is excessive. . . . Spectators not only tolerate violence, they sometimes encourage it."

The problems in sports pale in comparison to other current issues such as international conflicts or epidemics. However, the issues that are brought up by supporters and critics of sports provide society with an opportunity to compare an ideal world to the real world and perhaps find ways to improve the latter. *Sports and Athletes: Opposing Viewpoints* considers these and related questions in the following chapters: Do Sports Benefit Children? Should College Sports Be Reformed? Is Racial Discrimination a Problem in Sports? Is There Sexual Equality in Sports? Is Drug Use a Problem in Sports? In these chapters, the authors debate the role of sports in society and whether the expectations placed on sports can be achieved.

DO SPORTS BENEFIT CHILDREN?

CHAPTER PREFACE

Participation in youth sports can have a physical price. Four million children under the age of fifteen are injured each year while playing sports. These injuries can range from contusions to fractures to conditions such as "Little League elbow," a muscle and bone problem that can affect young pitchers. In more extreme, but generally rare, cases, a sports-related injury can lead to death. In her book *Little Girls in Pretty Boxes: The Making and Breaking of Elite Gymnasts and Figure Skaters*, Joan Ryan writes about two girls who died as a result of gymnastics training and competition— one because of an eating disorder, the other due to injuries sustained after falling off an apparatus.

Sports advocates acknowledge that while injuries do occur in gymnastics and other sports, the overall benefits outweigh any dangers. In an article in *Synapse*, the student publication of the University of California at San Francisco Medical School, Ellen Kuwana writes, "As a result of my involvement in gymnastics, I tried to eat healthy food, work out regularly . . . I was a healthier person because I was a gymnast." Kuwana also argues that most gymnasts participate recreationally and do not face the same problems as competitive gymnasts.

In many cases, injuries to young athletes can be reduced or minimized through the use of protective equipment and the watchful eyes of parents and coaches. However, not all observers believe that every injury can be prevented. A report for the Institute for the Study of Youth Sports on the causes and misconceptions of pediatric sports injuries contends, "It is speculative and premature to suggest that injuries would not have occurred had the circumstances been ideal. The intuitive belief that up to one-half of pediatric athletic injuries are preventable must be substantiated by identified risk factors and effective interventions."

Youth sports offer physical benefits but can also involve risks. In the following chapter, the authors consider whether sports are beneficial to children.

| "When children engage in sports, they learn about taking turns with their teammates, sharing playing time, and valuing rules."

SPORTS CAN BENEFIT CHILDREN

Marty Ewing

In the following viewpoint, Marty Ewing argues that sports can help children develop morally and socially. Ewing asserts that participation in sports improves self-esteem and teaches children about fair play and the difference between right and wrong. However, Ewing contends, children can benefit from sports only if their parents and coaches offer encouragement, constructive criticism, and moral instruction. Ewing is an associate professor of kinesiology at Michigan State University in East Lansing, Michigan, and a staff member of the Institute for the Study of Youth Sports, a special unit at Michigan State University that researches the effects of participation in youth sports.

As you read, consider the following questions:

1. According to Ewing, how is self-esteem developed?
2. What makes coaches' feedback effective in helping athletes develop skills, according to the author?
3. In Ewing's view, at what point do parents and coaches stop supporting fair play?

Reprinted from Marty Ewing, "Promoting Social and Moral Development Through Sports," *Spotlight on Youth Sports*, Fall 1997, by permission of the Michigan State University Institute for the Study of Youth Sports. *References in the original have been omitted from this reprint.*

For most people the development of social roles and appropriate social behaviors should occur during the childhood years. Physical play between parents and children, as well as between siblings and/or peers, serves as a strong regulator in the developmental process. Physical play may take the form of chasing games, rough housing or wrestling, or practicing sport skills such as jumping, throwing, catching, and striking. These activities may be competitive or non-competitive and are important for promoting social and moral development of both boys and girls. Unfortunately, fathers will often engage in this sort of activity more with their sons than their daughters. Regardless of the sex of the child, both boys and girls enjoy these types of activities.

THE IMPORTANCE OF PHYSICAL PLAY

Physical play during infancy and early childhood is central to the development of social and emotional competence. Researchers have reported that children who engage in more physical play with their parents, particularly with parents who are sensitive and responsive to the child, exhibited greater enjoyment during the play sessions and were more popular with their peers. Likewise, these early interactions with parents, siblings and peers are important in helping children become more aware of their emotions and to learn to monitor and regulate their own emotional responses. Children learn quickly, through watching the responses of their parents, that certain behaviors make their parents smile and laugh while other behaviors cause their parents to frown and disengage from the activity. If children want the fun to continue, they engage in the behaviors that please others. As children near adolescence, they learn through rough-and-tumble play that there are limits to how far they can go before hurting someone (physically or emotionally), which results in termination of the activity or later rejection of the child by peers. These early interactions with parents and siblings are important in helping children learn appropriate behavior in the social situation of sport and physical activity.

Children learn to assess their social competence (i.e., ability to get along with and acceptance by peers, family members, teachers and coaches) in sport through the feedback received from parents and coaches. Initially, children are taught "you can't do that because I said so." As children approach school age parents begin the process of explaining why a behavior is right or wrong because children continuously ask, "why?" Similarly, when children engage in sports, they learn about taking turns with their teammates, sharing playing time, and valuing rules.

They understand that rules are important for everyone and without these regulations the game would become unfair. The learning of social competence is continuous as we expand our social arena and learn about different cultures. A constant in the learning process is the role of feedback as we assess the responses of others to our behaviors and/or comments.

In addition to the development of social competence, sport participation can help youth develop other forms of self-competence. Paramount among these self-competencies is self-esteem. Self-esteem is how we judge our worthiness and indicates the extent to which an individual believes her/himself to be capable, significant, successful and worthy. Educators have suggested that one of the biggest barriers to success in the classroom today is low self-esteem. Children are coming to our schools and sport teams with low self-esteem.

SPORTS AND SELF-ESTEEM

Self-esteem is developed through evaluating our abilities and by evaluating the responses of others to us. Children actively observe parents' and coaches' responses to their performances looking for signs (often nonverbal) of approval or disapproval of their behavior. No feedback and criticism are often interpreted as a negative response to the behavior. Within the sport arena, research has shown that the role of the coach is a critical source of information which influences children's self-esteem. Little League baseball players whose coaches had been trained to use a "positive approach" to coaching (more frequent encouragement, positive reinforcement for effort and corrective, instructional feedback) had significantly higher self-esteem ratings over the course of a season than children whose coaches used these techniques less frequently. However, the most compelling evidence supporting the importance of coaches' feedback was found for those children who started the season with the lowest self-esteem ratings. In addition to evaluating themselves more positively, low self-esteem children evaluated their coaches more positively than did children with higher self-esteem who played for coaches who used the "positive approach." Moreover, 95 percent of the youth who played for coaches trained to use the positive approach signed up to play baseball the next year compared with 75 percent of the youth who played for untrained adult coaches.

The importance of enhanced self-esteem on future participation cannot be overlooked. A major part of the development of high self-esteem is the pride and joy that children experience as their physical skills improve. (As adults we experience the same feelings when our boss compliments us on a job done well!) Children will feel good about themselves as long as their skills are improving. However, if children feel that their performance during a game or practice is not as good as that of others, or as good as they think mom and dad would want, they often experience shame and disappointment. Some children will view mistakes made during a game as failure and will look for ways to avoid participating in the task if they receive no encouragement to continue. At this juncture, it is critical that adults (parents and coaches) intervene to help children interpret the mistake or failure. Children need to be taught that a mistake is not synonymous with failure. Rather, a mistake means a new strategy, more practice, and/or greater effort is needed to succeed at the task.

Because children often use social comparison as a way of determining their ability in sport, the highly visible arena of youth sports provides children with many opportunities to determine their ability compared with others on their teams. Unfortunately, given the influence of other factors such as maturation and previous knowledge of a sport on one's ability to perform a sport skill, children often reach incorrect conclusions about their abilities. Thus, the role of parents and coaches becomes significant in helping children interpret the failure.

Perceiving Competency

The development of self-esteem and perceptions of competence are not as simple as providing only positive feedback. The role of coaches' feedback, while critical, is complex. For example, among 13 to 15 year old female softball players, skill development was the primary contributor to positive changes in self-perceptions of ability. However, certain coaching behaviors also influenced perceptions of self-esteem during practice situations. Specifically, players who received more frequent positive feedback or no feedback in response to desirable performances during practice scored lower in perceived physical competence, while players who received more criticism in response to performance errors had higher perceptions of competence. Although these results appear contradictory to interpretations of the roles of positive and negative reinforcement, Thelma Sternberg Horn attributed these findings to the specific nature of the comments. Positive reinforcement statements given by coaches were often unrelated to players' skill behaviors. That is, statements were not responses to desirable skill techniques and behaviors, but rather were more general (e.g., "good job, Sally" rather than "good job, Sally, on using two hands to catch the ball"). Coaches' use of criticism was often a direct response to a skill error and usually contained skill relevant information on how to improve (e.g., "That's not the way to hit a ball, Jill! Put both hands together and keep your elbows away from your body"). Thus, the quality of coaches' feedback is critical to children's understanding of the feedback. Specifically, instructional content, rather than the quantity of the feedback, is the key to helping athletes develop skills and perceived competence.

Another issue related to social competence, particularly during the adolescent years, is how youth perceive their competence in an activity, including sport. Research has shown a significant relationship between physical competence, interpersonal skills, and peer acceptance. Boys and girls who believed that they were physically competent in sport were rated as having higher physical competence by their teachers. Those who believed that they were physically competent were also those who perceived themselves to be more popular with their peers, were competent in social relationships as rated by their teachers, and expected to be successful in interpersonal situations.

Finally, the development of high self-esteem is critical to help youth buffer the negative influences experienced by youth in today's society. For example, the Women's Sports Foundation has proposed that girls who have high self-esteem are less likely to become pregnant as teenagers and are more likely to leave an abusive relationship than girls with low self-esteem. When teenagers evaluate themselves in a positive way, they are more capable of saying "no" to drugs and gangs. High self-esteem will not guarantee that youth will make the right decisions, but it does provide a stronger basis for resisting the pressures that currently exist.

FAIR PLAY MUST BE TAUGHT

In addition to developing a positive sense of self, involvement in sport activities can assist children in learning what is right from wrong (i.e., moral development). Indeed, moral concepts of fairness support the very existence of the notion of sport. For youth to learn about fair play, sport activities must be designed to facilitate cooperation rather than just competition. One of the best ways that participation in sport can teach our children about fair play is through teaching the rules of the game and, more importantly, ABIDING by the rules during competition. If the league rules mandate that every member of the team plays for a specified amount of time (e.g., one-quarter of the game or a specified number of innings or minutes), parents and coaches should follow the rule without grumbling about what will happen when we HAVE to put Chris, a low ability athlete, in the game. Equally important is instilling the understanding that time and positions must be shared during the early learning periods. In addition, many of children's early experiences in informal and formal sports require that children serve as their own officials. Tennis players must call their own lines during competitions while pick-up games require that children call their own fouls. These games only continue peacefully to the extent that everyone cooperates to have a game and is fair in their officiating calls. If fair play is to be taught and learned, it is the responsibility of all those associated with the sport experience to help athletes learn and appreciate the concept of fair play.

TEAM SPORTS CAN BE BENEFICIAL

Many feel that there are significant benefits to team sports. One father said regarding his son's playing football: 'It keeps him off the streets. It teaches him discipline.' Others feel that playing on a team teaches a youth to work with others—a skill that could have lifelong benefits. Team sports also teach youths to follow rules, to be self-disciplined, to exercise leadership, and to deal graciously with both success and failure.

Awake! February 22, 1996.

Parents, coaches, and officials will undermine the learning of the concept of fair play if they are not consistent in their teaching and personal conduct. Most coaches and parents espouse the virtue of fair play until they perceive that the opponent is gaining an advantage or winning unfairly. Parents may even chastise the coach who abides by the rules and does not win, which sends a mixed message to youth about the importance of fair play. Journalists and broadcasters have fallen into the same trap of believing that the only worthy performance was that given by the winning team regardless of whether they abided by the rules or not. For example, broadcasters laud the cleverness of a team which is able to confuse the official and send a better free throw shooter to the line instead of the person who was fouled. Parents and coaches must help youth interpret the appropriateness of these behaviors in light of what is right and wrong.

The development of appropriate social behavior begins BEFORE children enter sports. Parents and siblings provide important information to infants, toddlers and young children about acceptable ways to respond to being frustrated. For example, children learn that biting, hitting, pinching and kicking are not acceptable ways to retaliate because (1) these actions hurt others and (2) the play often stops when children act inappropriately. Learning the limits to which one can go and still maintain the "game" is one way children learn how to interact successfully with other children.

THE OBLIGATIONS OF PARENTS AND COACHES

Participation in sport extends the learning of social competence by teaching children to cooperate with their teammates and opponents as well as abide by the rules. Without this cooperation the game will not continue. Parents and coaches must be persistent and consistent in teaching the value of cooperation.

Parents must provide opportunities to learn social competence to both their daughters and sons. Fathers, in particular, are often more involved in teaching social competence through physical activity and sport to their sons. The outcomes of a high level of perceived competence (i.e., enhanced self-esteem, higher perceptions of competence, and greater acceptance by friends) are equally important to both girls and boys.

Coaches can facilitate the development of social competence through the use of positive feedback. When teaching sport skills, coaches should provide plenty of instructional and encouraging statements. Children are going to make mistakes while learning and performing sport skills. The use of a positive approach to error correction will assure that children will want to continue to practice and will enhance self-esteem, particularly among youth who have lower self-esteem.

Sport provides numerous opportunities to teach moral principles. The key to children learning what is right and wrong starts with coaches and parents being consistent in their OWN behavior. Coaches and parents should:
• use situations that arise in sport as opportunities to teach WHY certain behaviors are right and others are wrong,
• talk about the importance of being honest,
• promote acceptance of responsibility for one's actions,
• teach children to respect one's teammates, opponents and officials.

> "Training and competition have
> become potential hazards to
> [children's] physical and emotional
> health."

SPORTS CAN HARM CHILDREN

Patricia Dalton

In the following viewpoint, Patricia Dalton maintains that children who participate in competitive sports are often asked to train and perform beyond their physical and emotional capacities. In her estimation, the amount of time required to succeed in sports can lead to a loss of key childhood experiences, such as socializing with friends and family. Dalton contends that parents, coaches, and doctors need to be aware of and reduce the physical and psychological risks that can occur in children as a result of an overemphasis on sports. Dalton is a clinical psychologist in private practice in Washington, D.C.

As you read, consider the following questions:

1. How have children's sports schedules changed, according to the author?
2. What was Jimmy Connors's reaction to his son's decision not to become a professional tennis player, as cited by Dalton?
3. According to Dalton, what is the "female-athlete triad"?

Reprinted from Patricia Dalton, "When Play Is No Fun," *The Washington Post National Weekly Edition*, August 5–11, 1996, p. 22, by permission of the author.

It was a thrilling and inspiring moment: U.S. gymnast Kerri Strug, in obvious pain, shrugging off an ankle injury and sprinting down the runway to guarantee Olympic gold for her team and her country. Her goal achieved, she collapsed to the mat, unable to walk. As a spectator, I marveled at her toughness. As a psychologist who counsels families and as the parent of three children who have played sports for years, I wanted to shout to the millions of kids watching on TV two weeks ago: This might not be good for Kerri—and it certainly isn't good for you.

I'm not as concerned about elite athletes as I am about the 20 million boys and girls who participate in sports across the country. You have to wonder how many parents and coaches will cite Strug's example to kids—get tough, shake it off, play through pain no matter how much it hurts. A tutor I know works with young gymnasts in Virginia who are home-schooled so they can put in a 40-hour practice week at the gym. One of the gymnasts, sitting with ice on her injured knee, asked the tutor to please tell her father that she wanted to quit gymnastics. She couldn't bring herself to tell him on her own.

BENEFITS AND DRAWBACKS

Clearly, young athletes derive real benefits from playing sports. Mine have, and so have many others I have watched on suburban basketball courts and soccer fields. They become more disciplined and confident. They learn to perform under pressure and deal with setbacks. They make new friends and learn to set goals. As I watched my daughter's high school basketball team play, I thought about how much more has become available to girls since the passage of Title IX, the federal legislation that mandated equal opportunity and funding for girls' and boys' sports. My Catholic girls' high school in Toledo, Ohio, didn't have a girls' basketball team, so I only played intramurals. It wasn't until I became an adult that I started playing in a league and learned how much I enjoy the sport.

The irony is that for girls as well as boys, training and competition have become potential hazards to their physical and emotional health. We all know that detrimental sports practices have existed for years—I can remember guys I knew in high school taking laxatives to make weight for wrestling matches. But it's obvious today that the time and pressure attached to competing have been ratcheted up several levels. And the people you would expect to be most concerned and sometimes alarmed, the parents, are often strangely silent.

Sports Affect Childhood

Kids used to start sports at later ages, had fewer practices and played shorter sport seasons. Year-round sports were unusual, except for elite athletes. Today, you would think many local athletes were in training for the Olympics to see their schedules. I know of parent-chauffeurs (I'm one of them during basketball season) who need a Filofax with 15-minute increments to keep up with all the practices and games. I've had parents confide to me that they're thrilled when practices are rained out and secretly hope that their kid's team won't win tournament games so the season will be over. Kids' sports can feel like a runaway train that can't be slowed down—even to parents who aren't all that ambitious for their kids.

How does all this pressure change the nature of childhood? In an eye-opening book on the downside of gymnastics and figure skating, *Little Girls in Pretty Boxes* by Joan Ryan, gymnastics coach Steve Nunno makes a statement that shows a remarkable ignorance of child and adolescent development. He says, "What did [Olympic gymnast] Shannon [Miller] give up [to do gymnastics]? She gave up nothing. . . . She'll be done with her career at 19 or 20 and will have the rest of her life to go to the movies with friends." He speaks as if childhood experiences can be put off indefinitely with no adverse effects. But child development experts, teachers and therapists know differently. Once that time is gone, it is gone forever.

Marie Winn, who has written persuasively about the changing nature of childhood, puts it this way in her book *Children Without Childhood*: "We are at the beginning of a new era. Once parents struggled to preserve children's innocence, to keep childhood a carefree, golden age. The new era operates on the belief that children must be exposed early to adult experience in order to survive. The age of protection has ended. An age of preparation has begun."

At no time is the human psyche more malleable than when physical growth is occurring. How children are treated and how they spend their time will have lifelong reverberations. Yet coaches and parents can be amazingly oblivious to adverse effects of training on their kids. I've seen coaches yell at kids, humiliate them, use expletives and in general get away with behavior in the name of winning that would not be tolerated in other settings. Children and teenagers have radar for the real reasons adults want them to compete: They can tell when something is truly for them, and when it is really for the gratification or glory of adults. This is not a small issue. The development of their sense of trust and their ability to empathize with others is involved, with real consequences for the quality of their lives and future relationships.

When someone questions whether this unswerving dedication to training is natural for a child, I've heard more than one parent say, "But he [or she] loves it." And sometimes the child really has taken the lead. But a young person may also seem to love a sport simply because she's known little else. It must be remembered that kids depend on parents and want to please them, especially at young ages. What parents want and what their offspring want can get very mixed up. *The New England Journal of Medicine* carried an article that coined a term, "achievement by proxy," to describe parents and coaches seeking to experience a child athlete's success vicariously.

PROBLEMS ARISE IN ADULT LIFE

As I watch kids compete, the bumper sticker "Are we having fun yet?" sometimes comes to mind. If people don't have fun during their school years, it's not likely to happen when they get older. The stores of vitality that give our lives meaning and color and interest are formed when we are boys and girls. If school and sports practices take up all their time, when do kids daydream, read books, fool around, hang out with friends, date and pursue interests? Much less spend time with their families or eat meals together? What would they be doing and learning and experiencing with all that time spent in practice? Is the trade-off worth it?

CHILDREN ARE TREATED AS ADULTS

Many aspiring young gymnasts devote nearly all of their time to the sport and may thereby suffer from social isolation and a lack of opportunities for social development. At the elite level, gymnasts work out on average 30 to 45 hours per week. They may leave home before the age of 12 to train and in some cases are adopted by their coaches. At every competitive level, critical coaching with the goal of winning is paramount. Young female gymnasts begin traveling extensively and staying in hotels and are often expected to behave as independent adults at a time when they may not even have entered puberty. Parents and coaches often attribute a child's overtraining to the child's enthusiasm and love for the sport, but this may be little more than self-deception and an abrogation of adult responsibility.

Ian R. Tofler et al., *New England Journal of Medicine*, July 25, 1996.

One way to answer that question is to do follow-ups on the athletes themselves later in life, to see how they are doing. I recall a woman I once saw in couples therapy who had been a competitive swimmer as a child. One issue in their marriage was her work schedule, which her husband felt didn't leave them enough time together. It didn't bother her. It was clear to me that she had learned early on the habit of hard work and long hours. She had just not learned how to relax. Her husband finally left the marriage.

Another follow-up approach is to question former athletes: Would you do it again? Jimmy Connors has said that he is relieved that his son did not want to become a professional tennis player. He said, "In my heart I don't want him to do it. This is not a normal life."

PARENTS SHOULD PROTECT CHILDREN

Parents need to be willing to ask their child directly: Do you want to quit? Sometimes the answer is simple—it's yes or it's no. The response can be more complicated for kids who have been so immersed in a sport that they lack other interests. It can be even harder to quit when they're winning, even if there is little joy left in the sport. There is a great deal of prestige and narcissistic gratification—some of it good—that is showered on winners in our society. But we are talking about serious stakes: being a whole person who can enjoy life without the adrenaline rushes that fame can provide, however unpredictably. Very few of us are destined to be in the limelight all our lives.

Parents are the first and most important line of defense against the risks of sports to their children. The match of particular child and particular sport as well as coach needs to be considered. In general, the riskiest sports are the individual ones. Other risk factors include starting at a young age; striving for a specific and slender body type and shape; training rigorously year-round; and competing at the elite or scholarship level. Certain personality types are also at higher risk, especially compliant, stoic, perfectionist children. It must also be remembered that when a family or athlete has made unusual or excessive sacrifices for the training, or really needs that scholarship money, it can be harder for the child to walk away, in spite of the price he or she is paying.

Parents aren't the only ones who bear responsibility. Coaches do too. They need to understand that, by virtue of their age and position of power, they can abuse their charges, especially when the young athlete cannot or will not quit. Likewise, school principals and college administrators also bear some responsibility. They owe it to their students to find out what is going on with their sports programs, to address any serious problems and to rectify them or relieve the coach of his or her duties if necessary.

SPORTS CAN BE PHYSICALLY DANGEROUS

Medical doctors also can take an active role in advocating for the young athlete's physical and emotional welfare. Doctors do screening physicals and treat injuries and training-related conditions. They are in a good position to pick up early warning signs and prevent potential serious problems. For instance, pediatricians and gynecologists sometimes treat girls for amenorrhea (dysfunction in the menstrual cycle), one of three conditions known as the "female-athlete triad," which also includes eating disorders and osteoporosis.

Too often, young athletes are encouraged to play when they should rest. Young athletes with injured joints shouldn't be put in a brace or receive cortisone shots so they can return to the playing field; this risks further and more serious injury. Orthopedic surgeons should remember—as the best do—that they are doctors first and foremost, and sports doctors second.

In March 1996, Nike ran an ad campaign sure to catch the attention of parents. In it, a series of healthy, clear-eyed teenage girls stated, "If you let me play sports . . ." and then listed the advantages: less likelihood of teenage pregnancy and substance abuse, higher grades and SAT scores, and presumably a better start in adult life. I couldn't help but imagine a different, cautionary ad that would start, "If you make me play sports . . ."

Maybe the best guideline for all of us is the wisdom of the ages. As Samuel Johnson said many years ago, "Allow children to be happy in their own way: for what better way will they ever find?"

"Most analysts agree that black youth's intense focus on athletics is socially perverse."

A PREOCCUPATION WITH SPORTS IS DETRIMENTAL TO AFRICAN-AMERICAN YOUTH

Salim Muwakkil

In the following viewpoint, Salim Muwakkil argues that too many young African Americans regard professional sports as a potential career, despite the fact that only one out of every fifty-thousand African-American men ever participate in a professional sport. As a result, Muwakkil contends, these youths do not consider other jobs that offer more realistic opportunities for financial security. In addition, Muwakkil maintains that selecting black athlete role models such as Michael Jordan and Emmitt Smith, who are largely apolitical, does not encourage black youth to work toward improving the communities in which they live. Muwakkil is a senior editor at In These Times, a liberal biweekly publication.

As you read, consider the following questions:

1. According to the poll cited by the author, what percentage of African-American teenagers in urban neighborhoods believe they can have a career playing sports?
2. In Muwakkil's view, why is the popularity of Michael Jordan not necessarily an indication of racial progress?
3. How should the African-American community contextualize athletic success, according to the author?

Reprinted from Salim Muwakkil, "Which Team Are You On?" In These Times, May 3, 1998, by permission.

Perusing Black Voices, a Web site dedicated to news of interest to African-Americans, I noticed that the top five stories highlighted errant Chicago Bear Alonzo Spellman, golf phenom Tiger Woods, disgraced ex-champ Mike Tyson, pious Green Bay Packer Reggie White and Golden State Warrior Latrell Sprewell, who infamously choked his coach. Black Voices' heavy focus on black athletes may have been skewed a bit by a coincidence of events. But there is no denying the inordinate prominence of ball players, fist swingers and fast runners in African-American culture.

In 1997, golfer Wood's victory in the Masters and the 50th anniversary of Jackie Robinson's desegregation of Major League Baseball catapulted an intense discussion of the effect of sports on race relations onto the front pages. This public visibility focused a discussion on the racial dimension of athletics and forced a general realization of extraordinary influence of sports in African-American society.

SPORTS AND SUPREMACY

Confronted historically by the manifold indignities of racist exclusion, blacks have long seen sports as a source of inspiration. In the first half of the twentieth century, the success of black boxing champions like Jack Johnson and Joe Louis, Olympic runner Jesse Owens and baseball's Robinson inspired parades and other demonstrations of race pride in African-American communities. "These athletes were refuting the 'Tarzan mentality' that white men could do anything better than blacks," says Alvin Poussaint, a Harvard Medical School psychiatrist. "The sports arena became a battleground against white supremacy." But now, Poussaint warns, "There is an overemphasis on sports in the black community. Too many black students are putting all their eggs in one basket."

A poll by Northeastern University's Center for the Study of Sport in Society found that 66 percent of black teenagers in urban centers believe they can earn a living playing sports. This is more than twice the percentage of young whites who hold such beliefs. Black parents also are four times more likely than white parents to believe that their children are destined for professional sports. Yet, according to Michael Messner, whose 1992 book, Power at Play, examines the powerful influence of sports in American culture, a black man has only a 1-in-50,000 chance of going pro.

Blacks are a dominant presence in our three national sports. Even though they make up only 13 percent of the U.S. population, a little more than 80 percent of National Basketball Association (NBA) players, 67 percent of the players in the National Football League (NFL) and 17 percent of Major League Baseball (MLB) players are black.

Yet even in these integrated workplaces, African-Americans are disproportionately shut out of the front offices. According to a survey by the Center for the Study of Sport in Society, African-Americans make up 20 percent of NBA, 21 percent of NFL and 15 percent of MLB management. "Despite well-intentioned efforts for diversity, white males still control most of our teams, front offices and athletic departments," says the center's director, Richard Lapchick.

The huge amount of money that sports superstars earn has brought the black athlete to "the top of the prestige order," says Harry Edwards, a sociologist at the University of California-Berkeley. The average annual salary in the NBA is $2 million, in the NFL it's $767,000, and in MLB it's $1.1 million. With celebrity endorsements, stars like Michael Jordan and Shaquille O'Neal earn as much as $50 million a year.

Is it any wonder so many young people want, as the Gatorade commercial puts it, to "be like Mike"? Indeed, dark-skinned Jordan's cultural omnipresence is a sign not only of how prominent sports have become in American life, but also of how corporations socialize the nation's youth. Sports metaphors now flavor our contemporary lexicon ("three-strikes," "level playing field," "slam dunk"), influence our vernacular gestures (high-fives, end-zone dances) and dictate our apparel (baseball caps, starter jackets, sneakers).

SUCCESS DOES NOT BENEFIT ALL BLACKS

But contrary to popular opinion, Jordan's wide acceptance is not necessarily the herald of a coming color-blindness in society or even of racial progress. The integration of sports is appealing because it promises better race relations through entertainment. But while blacks are generating billions of dollars in revenue, very little of that money filters down to the impoverished black communities where many pros start playing the game.

When media images of rich and famous black athletes are contrasted with the despair, crime and poverty that characterize too many African-American communities, is it any wonder that so many young blacks harbor "Hoop Dreams"? Most analysts agree that black youth's intense focus on athletics is socially perverse. While the civil rights struggle has forced open many more employment opportunities, African-American youth are too preoccupied with sports to utilize their expanded options. Indeed, those who wish to get ahead in other occupations often pay a high price. Tales of academically successful black students being accused of "acting white" and then being ostracized by their peers are legion.

ATHLETIC SUCCESS CAN BE DANGEROUS

Author John Hoberman argues that black leaders and intellectuals are downplaying a crisis. "The cult of black athleticism is emblematic of an entire complex of black problems, which includes the adolescent violence and academic failure that have come to symbolize the black male for most Americans," Hoberman writes in his 1997 book, *Darwin's Athletes: How Sport Has Damaged Black America and Preserved the Myth of Race.* Hoberman, a professor of Germanic Studies at the University of Texas, argues provocatively that the success of black athletes diverts the attention of African-American youth from academics to the playground.

"The whole problem here," he writes, "is that the black middle class is rendered essentially invisible by the parade of black athletes and criminals on television." This public visibility merely reinforces the notion—among blacks as well as whites—that African-Americans have physical gifts but lack mental capacity. The image of black male athletes as oversexed and feral, with violent tendencies just barely held in check by the rigors of athletic discipline, is a view that has its roots in slavery. But Hoberman says that it has become a racist tradition. Hoberman understands the compensatory motive driving some blacks to promote the superjock stereotype, but he is less forgiving of black intellectuals. While they readily condemn other forms of cultural exploitation, he writes, they "see stylish black athleticism as a kind of cultural avant-garde."

Darwin's Athletes stirred up quite a controversy. Hoberman's slash-and-burn prose style is partly to blame, but he's also a white author writing unsentimentally—and at times scathingly—about African-American culture. His critics say he gives too much credit to notions long debunked. They argue that ideas of savage blacks threatening cerebral whites have been relegated to the dust bin of history.

OPPOSITION TO HOBERMAN

Kenneth Shropshire wrote extensively about this subject in his 1997 book, *In Black and White: Race and Sports in America.* He characterizes Hoberman's efforts as part of the "multifaceted projected view of white intellectual superiority." Writing in *Sports Based Press,* an online "journal of the African-American athlete," Shropshire observes that Hoberman is so intent on constructing formulaic assessments, he misses the point "that many African-Americans, like whites, participate in sports not for some 'Hoop Dream' of pro success but for a simple love of the game. And at another level, sports serve as a vehicle or means of entering into a lucrative profession." Shropshire argues that Hoberman's book merely manifests white fears of black athletic domination.

BETTING AGAINST THE ODDS

The social forces that influence the sport socialization of African American youth are varied and complex. The mass media has a great impact in shaping the values and sports aspirations of American youth. It fills the minds of American kids with the notion that professional sports are attainable. The percentages of African American athletes playing professional baseball, basketball, and football are an overrepresentation of the percentage of African Americans in society. Currently, approximately 80% of the NBA, 60% of the NFL, and 25% of major league baseball are African American. However, only 12% of Americans are African American.

These statistics appear to convey the notion that African American opportunity exists in professional sport. However, the converse is true. Too many African American males are buying into the dream and are betting against the odds. They are foregoing the opportunity to earn a college degree to "go pro!" There are far too many casualties that bet against the odds and lose. Consequently, not having educational skills to fall back on makes the situation worse.

Gary A. Sailes, *Journal of African American Men*, Fall 1996/Winter 1997.

In truth, the fact that African-American athletes dedicate themselves to sports is no more problematic than when whites do. White girls starve themselves for figure skating, ballet and gymnastics. Their ice/stage/beam dreams are no less pathological than the dreams of black boys to play in the NBA. The same may be said of fanatical little leaguers (and their parents) buzzing about suburbia or the children of the now-famous "soccer moms." In short, black Americans' infatuation with sports is just part of a national romance.

Darwin's Athletes raises important issues. For example, Hoberman argues that the political apathy and oblivious individualism of most professional athletes are programmed by the structure of professional sports. Why else are current black athletes so apolitical? Why, given their huge salaries and numerical advantage, don't black pro football players like Emmitt Smith, Deion Sanders and Jerry Rice flex their considerable muscle and agitate for more black coaches and owners in the NFL, which has had just four black head coaches in its entire history? Why don't Michael Jordan and Shaquille O'Neal (whose combined salaries outstrip the Gross National Product (GNP) of some developing countries) create enterprises or foundations to help better conditions in black communities? "Arthur Ashe answered one such question by correctly asserting that advertisers want somebody who's politically neutered," Hoberman writes. "That black athletes have been willing to conform to this standard is borne out by their conspicuous political quiescence."

POLITICS AND ATHLETICS

Hoberman's arguments echo those made by many black critics of professional athletics, including Malcolm X, who in the early '60s regularly condemned the "sport and play" mentality encouraged by pro sports. His successors in the black power era cast black athletes as court jesters hired to entertain the white masses. When Tommie Smith and John Carlos raised their fists in the black power salute on the victory stand at the 1968 Olympics in Mexico City, they broke from that jester role and were widely applauded by the militant black youth of the era. Since then, the sentiments symbolized by that action have faded badly.

Thirty years later, the black athlete remains largely divorced from the struggles of African-Americans and ever more under the yoke of corporate America. But contemporary analysts of sports and African-American culture are less damning of black athletes than they were in the past. This revisionist critique ascribes more agency to black players than previous analyses, which often portrayed black athletes as little more than hapless flotsam tossed about by social forces.

African-Americans are not hapless victims of history, but they have been victimized by historical forces. Ignoring those patterns does little to eliminate them, and books like *Darwin's Athletes* help to add clarity and context. If African-Americans are to exploit the socio-economic options opened by varied civil rights struggles more fully, blacks must reduce the disproportionate allure of sports in their communities. Black leadership must contextualize athletic success by promoting other avenues to social status, intensifying the struggle for access to those avenues and better educating youth about those potholes on the road to the stadium.

Can I get a high-five on that?

"Why is it . . . not okay for black
kids to pursue athletic dreams worth
millions?"

A Preoccupation with Sports Is Not Detrimental to African-American Youth

William Raspberry

In the following viewpoint, syndicated columnist William Raspberry maintains that African-American teenagers are not harmed
by harboring dreams of athletic success. Despite the assertions
of some critics, Raspberry argues that African-American children do not sacrifice their education or ignore more achievable
goals because of their desire to excel in sports. On the contrary,
he asserts that these youth do not abandon academics because
they know they need to do well in school in order to receive
athletic scholarships. Raspberry also notes that young white athletes do not receive similar criticism for holding unrealistic expectations of athletic fame.

As you read, consider the following questions:
1. What percentage of positions in the National Basketball
   Association are filled by African Americans, according to
   statistics cited by the author?
2. In Raspberry's opinion, what false comparison regarding
   college athletes do John Simons and John Hoberman make?
   What would be a more realistic comparison, according to
   Raspberry?
3. According to the author, what notion does Hoberman fear
   will likely be assumed if black students achieve too much
   athletic success?

Reprinted from William Raspberry, "Suffering Through Sports," *The Washington Post National
Weekly Edition*, March 31, 1997, with permission; ©1997, Washington Post Writers Group.

Here's something I'll bet you didn't know. The athletic success of black superstars is hurting black America. I didn't know it either, but it must be so. Not only does the cover story of the March 24, 1997, *U.S. News & World Report* say so; I've just seen a book devoted to the thesis. Now all I need is for someone to explain it to me.

A Controversial Thesis

The two authors do try. John Simons, who wrote the *U.S. News* piece, notes that African Americans—13 percent of the population—comprise 80 percent of the slots in the National Basketball Association and 67 percent of the positions in the National Football League. But because the odds against any particular young athlete ever earning the big money paid to the likes of Michael [Jordan] or Shaquille [O'Neal] or Emmitt [Smith] or Deion [Sanders], young people who dream of athletic stardom are deluding themselves.

Worse, the time they spend on sports is time not spent on other more achievable goals. And all of it is compounded by the fact that the nonathletic rest of us pay such obeisance to the super athletes that it keeps tempting new generations of youngsters into putting all their eggs into the basket of professional sports.

Simons's piece is headlined "Improbable Dreams: African-Americans are a dominant presence in professional sports. Do blacks suffer as a result?"

John Hoberman is more direct in his book, *Darwin's Athletes: How Sport Has Damaged Black America and Preserved the Myth of Race*. "This sports fixation," says Hoberman, a professor of Germanic languages at the University of Texas, Austin, "damages black children by discouraging academic achievement in favor of physical self-expression, which is widely considered a racial trait."

A Flawed Theory

That line of reasoning has several problems, among them the assumption that if black children didn't chase dreams of athletic glory, they would turn their time and attention to academics. More likely, the reverse is the case. If young athletes know anything at all it is that they have to pull up their academic socks in order to get into college sports in the first place and keep them up in order to maintain athletic eligibility.

The major flaw in both the book and the cover story is the fallacy of the false comparison. The authors, both directly and implicitly, compare the academic performance of college athletes with that of nonathlete scholars. A more realistic comparison might be between two categories of the academically indifferent: those whose athletic abilities get them into college and those who, lacking both academic and athletic ability, don't even think about higher education.

ANALYZING BLACK SPORTS DOMINANCE

In response to an article like *Sports Illustrated*'s "Whatever Happened to the White Athlete?" blacks are likely to ask, Why is it whenever we dominate by virtue of merit a legitimate field of endeavor, it's always seen as a problem? On the one hand, some blacks are probably willing to take the view expressed in Steve Sailer's August 12, 1996, essay in *National Review*, "Great Black Hopes," in which he argues that black achievement in sports serves very practical ends, giving African-Americans a cultural and market niche, and that far from indicating a lack of intelligence, blacks' dominance in some sports reveals a highly specialized intelligence: what he calls "creative improvisation and on-the-fly interpersonal decision-making," which also explains "black dominance in jazz, running with the football, rap, dance, trash talking, preaching, and oratory." I suppose it might be said from this that blacks have fast-twitch brain cells. In any case, blacks had already been conceded these gifts by whites in earlier displays of condescension. But black sports dominance is no small thing to blacks because, as they deeply know, to win is to be human.

Gerald Early, *Nation*, August 10–17, 1998.

Another false assumption the authors seem to share is that the reason black youngsters work so hard at their game is that they all expect to become sports millionaires. Many—no doubt too many—do harbor unrealistic expectations. But I promise you that the senior who is a third-string forward on a middle-of-the-road collegiate basketball team is not playing and practicing hard because he expects to be drafted by the NBA. More likely, he simply loves the game. Indeed for him the game may be the one redeeming element in an otherwise difficult collegiate experience.

A DOUBLE STANDARD EXISTS

Would he be better off to spend more time in the books and less in the gym? Quite likely. My problem is with the position shared by Hoberman and Simons that the success of black superstars is bad for black America, not only because it distracts young athletes from their academics but also because it distracts the rest of us from presumably more legitimate achievers.

Isn't it interesting that the people who worry about athletic overemphasis on the part of young black boys never utter a peep about the young figure skaters and tennis players and gymnasts who not only miss much of the ordinary school experience but may actually leave home to be near the right coach or the right climate for their sport?

Why is it okay for these gifted (mostly) white youngsters to distort their lives in hope of a few moments of Olympic glory but not okay for black kids to pursue athletic dreams worth millions?

Hoberman's answer: Too much athletic success on the part of African Americans may feed the notion that they are naturally superior athletically—leaving open the notion that they are naturally inferior academically.

It's one thing to help our children see that they can, if they work at it, achieve important success in all sorts of endeavors. It's quite another to suggest that they should give up the success they already have. Whose interest would that serve?

"When we watch these Olympic athletes, let's hope many of the professional athletes are watching as well."

PROFESSIONAL ATHLETES ARE NOT GOOD ROLE MODELS

Armstrong Williams

In the following viewpoint, syndicated columnist Armstrong Williams contends that professional athletes are not ideal role models for children. He asserts that professional athletes frequently break laws or behave poorly but are forgiven because of their talents. The irresponsible and unrepentant behavior of some professional athletes sets bad examples for children, Williams argues. In comparison, amateur athletes should be admired, Williams asserts, because they love their sports and work hard, even though many of them, unlike their professional counterparts, will never receive money for their efforts.

As you read, consider the following questions:

1. What did boxer Riddick Bowe do at two fights and one press conference, as cited by the author?
2. What message are children receiving when professional athletes are repeatedly forgiven for their bad behavior, according to Williams?
3. In the author's view, how is value determined in modern society?

With the 1996 Summer Olympics beginning in Atlanta, the best that athletics has to offer will be on display. For these few weeks, many athletes who otherwise remain anonymous to much of the American public, despite their dedication and achievement, will have just a few minutes to show their skill and ability.

A platform dive, a gymnastics tumbling routine and a javelin toss may only take seconds, but these athletes have been training for years for these few seconds—and we don't know who they are.

SOME PROFESSIONAL ATHLETES ARE POOR ROLE MODELS

Instead, the athletes who are held as role models by our children are those who secure the large shoe contracts and the high-profile television endorsements. These are the names that we know and these are the names that our children know and wish to emulate—but are these the athletes our children should regard as role models?

Consider what has been happening in the world of sports.

In three fights, heavyweight champion Riddick Bowe has punched an opponent during a press conference, he has punched an opponent during a fight after that man was already down on the canvas on one knee, and in July 1996 his entourage attacked his opponent after the conclusion of a fight, producing a disgraceful and dangerous free-for-all in Madison Square Garden that was nationally televised on HBO.

Dallas Cowboy wide receiver Michael Irvin has pleaded no contest to charges related to a rendezvous with two topless dancers in a room full of drugs in some cheap hotel. Please bear in mind that this man is married with children.

Former professional baseball pitcher Steve Howe, already removed from the sport because of substance abuse, tried to board an airliner with a loaded gun.

And this list could go on and on . . .

ATHLETES ARE TOO EASILY FORGIVEN

Almost weekly, some professional athlete crosses the line and either breaks the law or just embarrasses himself, his teammates and his sport with his behavior. Yet we continue to pay these athletes huge salaries and we continue to forgive their actions, because of their ability to perform in the sporting arena.

The message we send these men is readily received by our own children: If you can play a sport well, you will be excused. If you can play a sport well, you will be treated differently. If you can play a sport well, you will get paid well and you can live by a set of rules just for athletes.

As many athletes continue to behave beyond both legal and ethical bounds and are forgiven and even rewarded, our children believe that this is just, and they wish to become athletes themselves, so they can break the rules without recrimination.

"OKAY.... I'LL SWAP YOU TWO DRUG USERS AND A GAMBLER FOR ONE DRUNK DRIVER AND AN ACCUSED DOUBLE-MURDERER...."

Bob Gorrell/Richmond *Times Dispatch*. Reprinted with permission.

But there's more . . .

The National Basketball Association's free-agent signing period for 1996 started, and many of the league's best players were able to seek new deals with new teams. In other words, these players were able to test the market to determine their worth.

All the signings are not done, but from what we have seen so far, close to $1 billion in contract agreements will be spent on a very few special players. Michael Jordan will make at least $25 million for one year. Alonzo Mourning will make more than $100 million over a seven-year period, and his new teammate Juwan Howard is not far behind. [Howard's deal was ruled invalid, and he re-signed with Washington.]

UNBELIEVABLE SALARIES

It is unbelievable that anyone can receive this amount of money to play a sport, but we have now entered the age of the $100 million player. And is anyone asking what impact this is having on our children?

In a society where value is determined by how much money

you make, how much more important is an athlete in the eyes of children than a teacher, a police officer, a minister or parents who don't make in a year what many of these athletes make in a single game? Or how much more important is an athlete making $25 million a year than the President of the United States, who only makes $200,000?

What exactly are we teaching our children to value when we pay athletes these extraordinary salaries, and then allow many of these same athletes to break rules without punishment?

AMATEUR ATHLETES ARE BETTER ROLE MODELS

The world of professional sports is in danger of tumbling out of control, and with it many of our children may be lost as well.

But during the 1996 Summer Olympics, we have a chance to watch many athletes we have never seen before and never heard of, but who would be much better role models for our children.

Many of these athletes have to hold down jobs and practice when they have the chance. Many have become world-class performers without endorsements and with very little financial support. Many work at their sport simply for the love of the sport, having no huge monetary payoff waiting for them should they perform well.

So when we watch these Olympic athletes, let's hope many of the professional athletes are watching as well . . . and let's hope they learn something.

> "The heroism found in sports . . . is quite different from that of everyday people."

ATHLETES SHOULD NOT BE EXPECTED TO BE ROLE MODELS

Stephen D. Mosher

In the following viewpoint, Stephen D. Mosher contends that it is unrealistic and unfair to expect athletes to serve as heroes and role models for the rest of society. He argues that while the talent of certain athletes, such as Tiger Woods, may be heroic, this does not mean that such heroism is applicable to the lifestyle of the typical fan. In fact, according to Mosher, it is unwise to believe in the nobility of athletic competition since many of the participants behave poorly and since many team sports may foster negative social values. Mosher is an associate professor of exercise and sports sciences at Ithaca College in Ithaca, New York.

As you read, consider the following questions:

1. How did the Puritans view sports, according to Mosher?
2. According to the author, how do male athletes differ from male nonathletes?
3. In Mosher's view, why is Pete Rose a tragic figure?

Reprinted from Stephen D. Mosher, "Where Have All the Heroes Gone?" This article was written for and originally appeared in the Winter 1998 issue of the *Ithaca College Quarterly*, published by Ithaca College in Ithaca, New York, and is reprinted here with permission.

In the opening scenes of Robert Redford's *The Natural*, Roy Hobbs's father teaches his son how to pitch a baseball but also warns him, "You have a gift, Roy. But if you rely too much on your gift, you'll fail."

During one of the endless bus rides through the North Carolina League in *Bull Durham*, veteran catcher Crash Davis tells rookie Nuke Lalouche, "You don't respect yourself, which is your problem; but you don't respect the game, and that's my problem."

A LACK OF SPORTS HEROES

When we survey the contemporary American sport landscape, we are struck by the almost never-ending displays of immaturity (the frustrated American Olympic men's ice hockey team trashing their hotel rooms in Nagano in 1998), shameless self-promotion (the National Basketball Association/Women's National Basketball Association's [NBA/WNBA's] two-ball fiasco during the 1998 all-star weekend), blatant profit taking (Wayne Huizenga's dismantling of the Florida Marlins less than two weeks after they won the 1997 World Series), elitist protectionism (the Professional Golfers' Association [PGA], trying to prevent Casey Martin from joining its ranks by claiming that walking is integral to golf), overtly racist slurs (Fuzzy Zoeller's comments on Tiger Woods's eating habits and several incidents in the National Hockey League [NHL]), and personal violence (Latrell Sprewell's attack on Golden State basketball coach P.J. Carlesimo).

We ask ourselves: Where have all the heroes gone? Where is the nobility of sport? Who holds true to the ideals of the game? Who cares about sportsmanship and playing fair? Is it all just about winning?

The best athletes we can come up with to be role models for our children are those like Cal Ripken Jr. and Tara Lipinski. What exactly does Ripken do to have earned his hero status? Go to work every day and do his job just like countless other citizens? What advice for living life can come from the mouth of Lipinski? She's not even 16, has spent over half of her life skating, and already she's writing her *second* autobiography?

They are, however, reminders that celebrity is not fame. Moreover, the most honest athlete today may be Charles Barkley, who insists, "I am not a role model!". . .

LOOKING BACK AT AMERICAN SPORTS

Wherever did we come up with the belief that sport builds character or that it teaches us teamwork and how to be "good sports," how to be modest in victory and gracious in defeat? We must understand this before we can even ask our athletes to be our heroes.

Sport has not always been considered a good thing in American life. The Puritans, in their attempt to reform the Church of England, sought to squelch virtually all forms of organized rituals, holy days, pageantry, symbols, and play associated with the Roman Catholic church. Sporting pastimes in early America involved gambling (horse racing, bowling), violence (gouging, cockfighting), or both (boxing); all those directly connected with Catholic holidays were discouraged. However, the Puritans did approve "lawful" sport that could "refresh the spirit" or better prepare people to fulfill their religious duties. Lawful sports included fishing, hunting, and swimming. Children's play was also tolerated.

ATHLETES ARE NOT EXEMPLARY

No matter how one wants to define character, athletes very likely have no more of it than members of any other group. Some athletes are wonderful people, some are out-and-out thugs, and most of them are average folks. I have heard it said that sports reveals character. I would qualify that contention and say that sports reveals *athletic* character, the person's character on the field of competition. The athlete might be very different somewhere, or everywhere, else.

Robert S. Griffin, *Sports in the Lives of Children and Adolescents: Success on the Field and in Life,* 1998.

Nonetheless, the sporting traditions of the citizenry remained impossible to fully regulate. These activities were the province of the poor, the working class, children, and single, young men. But starting in the 1850s, as an outgrowth of the Second Great Awakening, social reformers again sought to govern the recreation of the greater society. Catharine Beecher's concept of womanhood—the "cult of domesticity"—and Thomas Higginson's concept of manhood—"muscular Christianity"—were the first sports-specific manifestations of this movement. The ideas gained momentum because advances in science, medicine, and technology, as well as the move away from an active agrarian lifestyle, meant that people no longer had physical activity, with its side perks of endurance and stamina, built into their daily lives. People were becoming sedentary.

For the first time in modern history, sport was seen to serve a purpose in developing the character of both boys and girls. Sport and physical exercise would assist girls in becoming healthy homemakers and nurturers and would prepare boys to enter the professional world. Basketball itself was invented by Dr. James Naismith, who'd been charged with creating a game that could be played indoors during the winter and would embrace all of the ideals of the Muscular Christian movement regarding teamwork, self-sacrifice, obedience, self-control, and loyalty.

The mottoes of the play movement organizations reveal volumes about their underlying purpose: "Mind, Body, Spirit" (YMCA), "Wohelo"—Work, Health, Love (Campfire), "Be Prepared" (Girl and Boy Scouts), "Head, Heart, Hands, Health" (4-H). The pledges of these movements are even more revealing. 4-H's pledge is *I pledge/My Head to clearer thinking,/My Heart to greater loyalty,/My Hands to larger service, and/My Health to better living,/for my club, my community, my country, and my world.* Even Little League Baseball has its own reformist pledge and motto: "Character, Courage, Loyalty."

SPORTS AND SOCIAL CLASS

Perhaps the most important key to understanding the problem of asking athletes to be role models is found in the modern Olympic movement. There is no doubt that the ideals of amateurism established in Britain at the end of the 19th century and promulgated through the Olympic Games served to separate people by social class. Many people fondly talk of the nobility of the "taking part," the "inclusion of all" in the Olympics. But the amateur code actually sought to prevent the working class from corrupting the sporting diversions of the wealthy. Simply put, the requirement that competitors be amateurs meant those who had to work for a living could not compete. Consequently, the "civilized gentlemen" of the ruling elite were able to exclude from sport virtually anyone they wanted.

In America, the self-described classless society, amateurism was met with some initial resistance (the early days of college sport were full of paid players and pseudostudents), but slowly took hold in the middle class. The morality of privilege, however, had little influence among those who were born to poverty and struggle or were immigrants; sport soon took on the looks of its new practitioners and was no longer cloaked simply in hunting suits and riding boots.

To expect sports as they exist today to teach children to play games, become physically healthy, and also build character may be unrealistic. In fact, the results of sport participation fall far short of these expectations. Competitive sports actually have little effect on the development of positive social characteristics. Research shows that competitive team sports are more likely to teach children that "winning is the *only* thing" and that "the end justifies the means" rather than that hard work, dedication, and self-sacrifice are the true payoffs. There are no convincing data to support the belief that sport prevents juvenile delinquency or reduces drug abuse. There are, however, data that suggest that male athletes develop a view of gender superiority that may explain their higher rates of promiscuity and sexual abuse than those of nonathletes. (There is also ample research showing that athletes are significantly less altruistic than nonathletes.) It is certainly quite clear that in most high schools varsity athletes enjoy higher status than those students who excel in art, music, and even academics.

Understanding Sports Heroism

We are quick to condemn the behavior of Mike Tyson, as if we can separate the champion boxer from the street thug. We are disgusted by Latrell Sprewell's assault on an authority figure, as if P.J. Carlesimo's long history of bullying players is irrelevant. On the other hand, Arthur Ashe was certainly a hero, but it wasn't tennis that led him to fight for greater awareness of HIV/AIDS, write *A Hard Road to Glory*, or protest the racist government in South Africa. Muhammad Ali was certainly a warrior king, but it wasn't boxing that prompted him to sacrifice his career when he said, "I ain't got no quarrel with them Viet Cong."

The heroism found in sports is powerful, legitimate, and sometimes even magical, but it is a heroism that is quite different from that of everyday people. When Gatorade urges us to "Be like Mike," are they talking about Michael Jordan the basketball player, the husband and father, or the endorser of a company that has been accused of exploiting child labor in the third world? Are we really supposed to believe Andre Agassi when he says for Canon cameras, "Image is everything"? Earl Woods has said that his son is literally capable of *saving the world*. Isn't it enough to simply marvel at Tiger's heroic golfing ability? Why do we insist on turning this young man's good manners into heroism?

Heroism in Baseball

During the summer of 1998, major league baseball reclaimed some of its lost dignity through the homerun-hitting achievements of Mark McGwire and Sammy Sosa. The duo was presented to the American public via a media frenzy seldom seen in

American sports. Sosa, leading the long-suffering Chicago Cubs to the playoffs, displayed graciousness throughout the late summer as McGwire, playing for the out-of-contention St. Louis Cardinals, led the pursuit on Roger Maris' record as well as Babe Ruth's ghost.

McGwire's personal triumph on September 8, 1998, ended with a fireworks display, the embracing of his rival Sosa and the Maris family, and the hoisting of his son in a fatherly celebration. The media constructed such a positive view of McGwire as a hero that it overwhelmed the controversy of his use of performance enhancing (but not banned in baseball) drugs.

Sosa's personal triumph, which was signified by his overwhelming victory in the voting for the National League's Most Valuable Player award, ended in national tragedy as his home country, the Dominican Republic, suffered massive loss of life and property at the hands of Hurricane Georges.

Sosa and McGwire, as well as the extraordinary team effort by the New York Yankees, so the media told us, had carried Major League Baseball all the way back to its "rightful place as the national pastime." Of course, all the media hype, myth and hero making could not prevent the 1998 World Series from achieving the lowest television rating *ever*. The question is begged: What good are heroes if no one is watching them?

SOME HEROES FAIL

One of the most tragic figures in recent American sport is Pete Rose. The ultimate symbol of hard work and determination overcoming a perceived lack of talent, Rose nonetheless remains the disgraced and fallen hero, clueless as to why he can't get into baseball's hall of fame on the basis of his heroic diamond feats alone. Rose's hubris really knows no limits. He would be well served to heed Crash Davis's advice: "You have to play this game with fear and arrogance." Rose, like so many of our celebrity athletes, has the arrogance but lacks the fear. Like those celebrities who refer to themselves in the third person, Rose—the self-proclaimed "Hit King"—places himself above the game. Also known as "Charlie Hustle," Rose betrayed those who depended on him when, as manager of the Cincinnati Reds, he gambled on baseball. Rose's greatest "hustle" was trying to convince the public he loved the game more than he loved himself. Rose still does not recognize that heroes must fear letting us down.

Roy Hobbs's home run at the end of *The Natural* brings us joy and hope, not because he saves the world but because he saves himself. Ray Kinsella eases our pain at the end of *Field of Dreams*, not because he demonstrates the moral superiority of baseball but because he finally has the chance to tell his father he's sorry.

Perhaps Cal Ripken Jr. is a hero. He certainly is a marvelous baseball player. But to ask him—or any other athlete—to be father to the nation is unfair. He has enough of a burden being father to his own children. For us to get anything more than that from him is simply a blessing.

| "It is impossible to ... not be aware
that there are more parents treating
their kids like miniature adults."

OVERDEMANDING PARENTS CAN MAR CHILDREN'S SPORTS EXPERIENCES

Mike Beamish

In the following viewpoint, Mike Beamish argues that some parents put too much pressure on their children to succeed in sports, leading to emotional and physical problems as the children reach adolescence. He acknowledges that many parents are able to place sports in the proper perspective, treating athletics as an opportunity for children to have fun and learn. However, Beamish contends, other parents ignore the rules and values sports are supposed to teach because of their own desire to see their children succeed and win. Beamish is a sports columnist for the *Vancouver Sun* and a guest writer for the British Columbia Amateur Hockey Association.

As you read, consider the following questions:
1. Why is Murray Costello glad that soccer enrollments are nearly equal to hockey enrollments, as cited by Beamish?
2. According to Beamish, what is the premise of youth leagues?
3. What amazed Rick Wolff when he worked for the Cleveland Indians, as cited by the author?

Reprinted from Mike Beamish, "Pushy Parents Need to Remember Sports Is Supposed to Be Fun!" *Vancouver Sun*, April 27, 1996, by permission of the *Vancouver Sun*.

While the death of a seven-year-old pilot in spring 1996 provoked much outrage and anger, Jessica Dubroff's tragedy is an example, albeit a bizarre and unimaginable one, of something at work across North America: the urge of parents to press, maybe even bully, a child to be the best.

TOO MUCH PRESSURE

Somehow, somewhere, faith in the simplicity of childhood has been lost. Average just isn't good enough when it comes to raising our children. It is impossible to spend much time around the playing fields and arenas of North America today and not be aware that there are more parents treating their kids like miniature adults. And as shocking as the Dubroff story of pushy, airheaded parenting may seem, to an increasing number of us, it sounds all too familiar. Such intense focus on over achievement is, it seems, a growing phenomenon among those who demand more of those who play.

Too much organization and adult pressure on child athletes can lead to a range of emotional and physical problems in the early teen years, doctors say. If anything, however, the situation could worsen, exacerbated by workaholism, heightened economic insecurity, stress and the pervasive need of some adults to bask in the reflected glory of their kids. With greater and greater rewards available to those who make it, when so many Canadians are desperately trying to hang on to what they already have, the result is parents seeking ever more control over their children's lives.

It is the style of this generation, a manic obsession with highly organized games, practices, structures and achievement. So we see more activities with coaches, referees and regimentation, and less creative, independent play in schoolyards, driveways and backyards. The parents who produce and direct their children's dreams associate down time, time alone, with falling behind.

TROUBLES IN YOUTH HOCKEY

Whether it seems to make sense or not, Canadian kids are encouraged to play hockey not only in winter, but in spring leagues, summer camps and hockey schools. "Without making too much of a generalization, hockey parents are more demanding of their kids than they've ever been," says Murray Costello, president of the Canadian Hockey Association. In Canada, minor hockey is the most prominent example of prodigy creation, because of the masses of kids and parents involved and the incredible rewards for the few who make it.

Of the 523,000 registered players in Canada, half of one per cent will reach the point of playing on a minor-league team, never mind the National Hockey League (NHL). Think of minor hockey as a lottery, then, with hundreds of thousands of parents believing their little meal ticket is the one who'll beat the odds. That's why high-performance summer hockey schools are growing fast—too fast for Costello, who is concerned about purely profit-motivated operators, and burnout. To him, the happy childhood mix of hockey, lacrosse and baseball, and those impromptu games in the street and backyard, owed as much to Wayne Gretzky's development as the arenas of southern Ontario. At present, the Canadian hockey system produces more competent players than ever before, but increasingly the truly great players come from someplace else. "When I hear that soccer enrollments are on the verge of passing hockey, I say to myself, 'Good, because that means more hockey players are going into dry-land training,'" Costello says. "There's a feeling that if the guy two doors down is sending his kid to hockey school, you should be, too. But I'm a strong believer that hockey players should be encouraging different skills, so that they come back in the fall refreshed. We see too many youngsters dropping out of hockey at 13 or 14."

"MICHAEL JORDAN EARNS $25 MILLION! WHAT ARE YOU DOING STUDYING? GET OUTSIDE AND SHOOT SOME HOOPS!"

Reprinted by permission of Harley Schwadron.

When 17-year-old Travis came to his dad and told him he wanted to quit hockey, his father, Mark, not only agreed, but he also understood. Mark is not, as he happily admits, a pushy father, but in the back of his mind was the thought that Travis might become the third generation of Howes in a Red Wing jersey. It was the chance for Mark Howe's eldest son to play for a good bantam rep team, as much as anything else, that made Howe sign as a free agent with Detroit in 1992. "Minor hockey is so much more of a business than when I played," Howe says. "There are good people out there, don't get me wrong. But my sense is the child's welfare is becoming less and less important. The focus should be on instruction and developing character. But you wonder about some of the coaches and parents today. There's so much backbiting and infighting, yelling and screaming."

Howe prided himself in not getting too caught up in it. But when Travis started to slide into the anonymous pack of his midget AAA team, the father watched his son's self-esteem go on the rocks under coaching and parental pressure more intimidating than any opposing player. And so, Mark Howe said no more, too much. "The bottom line is I never saw Travis smile when he played," Howe says. "It was like he was playing for Mike Keenan. When he decided he wanted to drop out, I supported his decision 100 per cent. Within a week, Travis was his old self. I felt I'd got my boy back again." Howe and his wife Ginger have vowed that their younger son, Nolan, should grow up and find hockey appealing as an outlet for fun and learning. "Ginger made me swear on a stack of bibles that I'd never take Nolan out of house league hockey," Mark says. [House league hockey is noncompetitive and recreational.]

COACHES IGNORE THE SYSTEM

An attitude of the times, the drive to be the best strikes at the great mass of house league players as well. There's no guarantee even there that life perspectives are necessarily crystal clear. Youth leagues start out with the premise that teams should be balanced fairly, so that, in theory, each player has an equal chance to participate and win a fair share of games. That's the way the system is supposed to work, but some coaches need remedial training in respecting the meaning of fairness. "We all know of the loopholes that are found and the politicking that takes place from year to year," says sports psychologist Rick Wolff, who writes a column in *Sports Illustrated for Kids*. Wolff, the father of three, has some good news for those Canadians who believe there is no limit to the insanity one encounters in minor hockey. When he worked for the Cleveland Indians, Wolff was amazed by the number of big leaguers who didn't want their kids exposed to the pressures of Little League. These were ballplayers who actively encouraged their kids into skateboarding, skiing, anything to distract them from the demands of baseball.

"It was very surprising," Wolff says, "because here are the best and brightest graduates of Little League telling me they find it a turn-off." Once professionals challenge the myth, critics feel free to question the necessity of the Vince Lombardi approach—"the winner is the only person who is truly alive"—and other canons from the high priest of competition. Wolff would like to think that Lombardi's tactics no longer dominate the thinking of coaches working with nine and 10-year-old kids, but the rejection of his methods is by no means universal.

"Unfortunately, too many coaches feel their mandate is to go out and win when every poll shows that 90 per cent of kids would prefer to play on a losing team rather than sit on the bench," Wolff says. "They just want to play."

PARENTS SOMETIMES LACK LIMITS

While the vast majority of parents probably have things in perspective, some accept the contortion of their kids' lives, right up until the point where the dream dies. The stereotype that all of minor hockey is a puck-black hole of ethical turpitude is wrong, yet it's amazing how grown men and women can complicate a simple game we so love.

Soccer is no different. There is no limit to the length some parents will go to, says Keith Liddiard, when they think their kids are destined for greatness. The executive director of the British Columbia (B.C.) Youth Soccer Association cites three cases in 1996 where parents allowed guardianship of their children to be legally transferred to families in other districts so their kids could play higher-calibre competition. "An oft-heard comment from parents is we shouldn't allow it," Liddiard says. "However, when it comes to my kids everybody appreciates a rule for the masses, but when it comes to their own kids they're not quite sure."

If a sport offers the wrong experiences or teaches the wrong values, then it has lost its purpose. And it's Chris Johnson's purpose to ensure that the winning of trophies and tournaments doesn't take over the real reasons why children compete—fun, friendships and skill acquisition. A physical educator and motivational speaker at Douglas College in New Westminster, Johnson talks to some of B.C.'s 60,000 volunteer coaches about fair play, drug abuse and ways to develop sensitivities in communication with young athletes.

Unfortunately, only about 1,000 provincial coaches have joined the B.C. coaching association and subscribe to its code of ethics. Obvious as it may seem, Johnson says parents spend considerably more time researching daycare than looking into the character and background of those who guide their children's lives on the playing field.

"We leave our most treasured possessions in the hands of people we know little about," he says.

Finally, one last truth: While there is an established code of conduct for coaches, Johnson says there needs to be another: "We're making progress in educating coaches, but who's educating the parents?" he asks.

| "If a coach is producing winners, his lack of education and compassion draws little attention, much less criticism."

INAPPROPRIATE COACHING CAN MAR CHILDREN'S SPORTS EXPERIENCES

Joan Ryan

Coaches who lack sufficient knowledge about their sports or who place too great an emphasis on winning can be detrimental to young athletes, Joan Ryan maintains in the following viewpoint. For example, Ryan contends that many coaches are not schooled in physiology and therefore ignorantly encourage excessive training that may lead to physical problems for the young athletes in their care. Furthermore, she claims, coaches are hired to develop successful athletes, which frequently means placing winning above concern for the children's well-being. Ryan is a sportswriter for the *San Francisco Chronicle* and the author of *Little Girls in Pretty Boxes: The Making and Breaking of Elite Gymnasts and Figure Skaters*, from which this viewpoint is taken.

As you read, consider the following questions:

1. According to the study by Anders Ericsson, cited by the author, how many hours per day can a top achiever in sports train arduously before ill effects occur?
2. What two requirements does Steve Nunno think all coaches should possess, as quoted by Ryan?
3. In the author's view, how would parents benefit from coaches' licensing?

Most coaches in the United States have no formal training in coaching. Most learn their sports as competitors, though not necessarily as elite competitors. Anyone can put an ad in the newspaper and declare himself a coach. "Jack the Ripper could walk off the street and coach your child," says Dr. Lyle Micheli, a pediatric orthopedist at Harvard Medical School and former president of the American College of Sports Medicine. "Some of the biggest offenders are the elite coaches. If they have to sacrifice seven kids to get one champion, some will do it." Micheli supports legislation that would require every coach from Little League on up to be certified, as they are in Canada, Australia and New Zealand. He'd like coaches to be educated in basic child psychology and physiology, which might make them less likely to enforce arbitrary weight goals that drive athletes to eating disorders or to demand unnecessary, potentially damaging, training. When a study found that swimmers who swam 10,000 yards a day performed no better than those who swam 5,000 yards, coaches still wanted their swimmers to go 10,000, clinging to the myth that more is always better.

A study by Dr. Anthony Kalinowski, a researcher at the University of Chicago, found that the more hours of training *over a lifetime* an athlete put in, the greater were his or her achievements—a finding coaches could use to bear out their belief that more is better. But what Kalinowski also found was that swimmers who competed nationally began training at age ten, while swimmers who competed on the Olympic team began training at age seven. Yet a Florida State psychologist, Dr. Anders Ericsson, found that the top achievers in sports, music or chess trained arduously for no more than four hours a day. After four hours, "you find a tremendous drop in mood, and a jump in irritability, fatigue and apathy."

UNDERSTANDING GIRLS' BODIES

Back when sports were exclusively male, coaches didn't need to know much more about physiology than how their own bodies and minds worked, which is vastly different from having to know the anatomy and psychology of children and teenage girls. Women have taken great strides in athletics over the last thirty years, but the coaching hasn't caught up. For the most part, girls still are coached on a male model without regard to bone density, menstrual cycles, growth plates and eating disorders, as well as the very real self-esteem issues that weigh on teenage girls. Research on young female athletes has been accumulating over the last decade, including that generated by a groundbreaking 1992 national conference called "The Female Triad" at which scientists addressed the physiological impact of intensive training on young female athletes. The conference, organized by sports medicine doctors and researchers, hoped to highlight their growing concern that early and excessive training could invite long-term damage. But few coaches in elite gymnastics or figure skating keep abreast of the latest research. Most aren't students of sports as much as they are students of winning.

SOME COACHES LACK ETHICS

Coaches are rewarded handsomely if they win. In addition to generous salary raises successful college coaches receive lucrative contracts from shoe companies and for other endorsements, media deals, summer camps, speaking engagements, country club memberships, insurance annuities, and the like. With potential income of college coaches approaching $1 million at the highest levels, the temptations are great to offer illegal inducements to prospective athletes or to find illicit ways to keep them eligible (phantom courses, surrogate test takers, altered transcripts). Because winning is so important, some coaches drive their athletes too hard, take them out of the classroom too much, and encourage them to use performance-enhancing drugs. They may also abuse their athletes physically. Verbal assaults by coaches are routine.

D. Stanley Eitzen, *Vital Speeches of the Day*, January 1, 1996.

It would be naïve to think that those who choose to coach female rather than male gymnasts do so because of a particular expertise or interest in female athletics. The fact is that girls' gymnastics is more popular and lucrative. "Girls are easier when they're young," says Kelli Hill, Dominique Dawes's coach. "Their body fat is low, so they still have a little boy's body. And boys aren't as disciplined. I coach girls the same age as my two sons, seven and eleven, and it's apples and oranges."

COACHES LACK CERTIFICATION

In a stab at upgrading its coaching ranks, USA Gymnastics has instituted voluntary certification for coaches through its new Professional Development Program, which offers courses on coaching technique and safety. "We are absolutely seeing that the coaches coming into our sports don't have physical education or education backgrounds," says Steve Whitlock, director of education and safety. "Over eighty percent are like myself. They came to the sport because they were athletes."

Steve Nunno says he wholeheartedly supports a certification process for coaches to screen out the unqualified people, who, according to Nunno, "could affect the lives of young Americans." He says the USA Gymnastics's new program is an excellent start, though he has not yet taken any of the courses himself. His views offer a good example of how fractured and contradictory the coaching community is on the issue. For example, Nunno suggests that a basic requirement for being a gymnastics coach should be a college degree. (He himself majored in business administration and earned a master's degree in sports administration, learning gymnastics first by competing, then by coaching under the likes of Bela Karolyi.) On second thought, Nunno says, the coaches should be required to have a two-year associate's degree. Or if the coach is young, then just a high school degree.

In the end, he comes up with two basic requirements: "I think first of all you have to have no criminal record. Second of all you have to be a good citizen."

Which would qualify most of America. The fact is, if a coach is producing winners, his lack of education and compassion draws little attention, much less criticism. The casualties of his coaching disappear so quickly we barely notice. In our microwave, Jiffy Lube, ATM, drive-through culture, it seems almost normal for a girl's athletic career to rise and fall in a blink. We're impatient for results, and gymnastics and figure skating feed our impatience with their production of ever-younger stars. The coach, who has to produce winners to thrive financially, must keep serving up new athletes, hoping one or two will make it and tossing away the rest. The girls are as disposable as everything else today, from cameras to contact lenses.

PARENTS IGNORE THE PROBLEMS

And though parents see their daughter's teammates disappearing one by one, they somehow never make the connection to themselves, envisioning some Hollywood version of success, something brilliant and lucrative. They're feeding at the same trough as the people who buy lottery tickets: though their chances of winning are laughably remote, *somebody* wins—and that provides enough hope to keep them buying tickets. For parents of young elite athletes, the end too often comes as a stunning disappointment, as if they've never heard the mounting rumble of the truck that finally hits them, though it is the same truck and the same blind corner that have crippled so many before them. The shock and grief were summed up perfectly by the mother who wept and raged for eight hours, pounding her fists against the walls of her rented Oklahoma City apartment after her unhappy, bulimic daughter quit gymnastics a year before the Olympics.

Coaches who claim they are paid to produce gymnasts and figure skaters and nothing more are betraying a trust implicit in the mentor-student relationship. Coaches of elite children's sports, by spending the bulk of every day with their athletes, can influence these children more than their parents or their teachers at school. The coaches become role models whether they want to or not. Their words and actions can profoundly affect the long-term physical and emotional health of their athletes, making the job too rife with the possibilities of abuse to allow it to continue unregulated.

Though the gymnastics and skating federations don't have the muscle to enforce even minimal coaching standards, they can make attendance at certain basic courses a requirement rather than a suggestion. Further, they can insist on the athletes' staying in school full-time until at least age sixteen; those who drop out would lose their eligibility to compete. Ultimately, it is up to the U.S. government to step in and require that every coach secure a license. Licensing won't eliminate the abusive coaches, but it will make it easier for a parent to insist on certain standards of behavior, knowing that the government backs them up.

CHILDHOOD SHOULD NOT BE DAMAGED

Whether we see any changes instituted to protect these young athletes hinges on our willingness to sacrifice a few medals for the sake of their health and well-being. Our obsession with winning, with dominating opponents and reveling in victory, is not considered a character flaw. On the contrary, few traits are more admired in this country than hard-driving ambition. And we expect sacrifices to be made in the name of great success. But when the sacrifices mean a childhood spent in the toils of physical and psychological abuse, the price is too high.

PERIODICAL BIBLIOGRAPHY

The following articles have been selected to supplement the diverse views presented in this chapter. Addresses are provided for periodicals not indexed in the *Readers' Guide to Periodical Literature*, the *Alternative Press Index*, the *Social Sciences Index*, or the *Index to Legal Periodicals and Books*.

Awake!	"Should I Join a Sports Team?" March 22, 1996. Available from Watchtower Bible and Tract Society of New York, Inc., 25 Columbia Heights, Brooklyn, NY 11201-2483.
Bill Dedman	"Where Children Play, Grown-Ups Often Brawl," *New York Times*, July 29, 1998.
D. Stanley Eitzen	"Ethical Dilemmas in American Sport: The Dark Side of Competition," *Vital Speeches of the Day*, January 1, 1996.
David Holmquist	"Will There Be Baseball in Heaven?" *Christianity Today*, January 10, 1994.
Barbara Kantrowitz with Adam Rogers and Allison Samuels	"Don't Just Do It for Daddy," *Newsweek*, December 9, 1996.
Frederick C. Klein	"In Gymnastics, Younger Isn't Always Better," *Wall Street Journal*, June 28, 1996.
Richard E. Lapchick	"Time to Invest in Urban Youth Sports," *Street & Smith's SportsBusiness Journal*, August 10–16, 1998. Available from 120 W. Morehead St., Suite 310, Charlotte, NC 28202.
William Raspberry	"The Disciplines of Basketball," *Liberal Opinion Week*, December 22, 1997. Available from PO Box 880, Vinton, IA 52349-0880.
Joan Ryan	"Role Models and Cautionary Tales," *Sporting News*, July 21, 1997. Available from 10176 Corporate Square Dr., Suite 200, St. Louis, MO 63132.
John Simons	"Improbable Dreams," *U.S. News & World Report*, March 24, 1997.
Joseph Sobran	"How Lucky to Have So Many Fathers," *Conservative Chronicle*, June 28, 1995. Available from PO Box 29, Hampton, IA 50441.
E.M. Swift	"Point After," *Sports Illustrated*, May 2, 1994.
Cynthia Tucker	"'Hoop Dreams Can Be Cruel Pipe Dreams,'" *Liberal Opinion Week*, March 27, 1995.

SHOULD COLLEGE SPORTS BE REFORMED?

CHAPTER PREFACE

In April 1998, the National Collegiate Athletic Association (NCAA) gave final approval to Proposition 62, a rule that allows Division I athletes, with the exception of first-year students, to hold part-time jobs. The rule took effect on August 1, 1998, amid debate over whether the NCAA's decision will help impoverished athletes or provide an easy way for athletic boosters to funnel money to star players.

Opponents to Proposition 62 argue that a key problem with the rule is that it allows athletic departments or boosters to arrange the jobs. Critics contend that boosters will offer star athletes jobs that involve little or no work at high wages, possibly surpassing the NCAA-imposed $2,000 annual limit. *Sports Illustrated* senior writer Rick Reilly writes that college athletes deserve money but receiving it from boosters is an ill-conceived solution. He observes, "This thing invites every cheat, influence peddler and game fixer right in the front door." Reilly and others assert that if the NCAA wants to provide athletes with spending money, it should permit monthly stipends or increase the monetary value of athletic scholarships.

Supporters of the proposition maintain that while the potential for abuse exists, college athletes are entitled to the opportunity—afforded to nonathletes—to earn money to watch a movie or go out to dinner. In a column in the *Austin American-Statesman*, Kirk Bohls writes, "Rules such as those prohibiting part-time work did nothing but penalize honest, law-abiding athletes who wanted to work, who don't take money under the table and who would like some extra spending money."

At the time of this writing, it remains to be seen whether Proposition 62 is a necessary change in college athletics or a misguided reform. In the following chapter, the authors examine the state of college sports and what, if anything, needs to be changed.

| "Four years of hard work and verifiable accomplishment in high school are negated by a 3½ hour, multiple choice test."

COLLEGE ENTRANCE REQUIREMENTS FOR ATHLETES ARE UNFAIR

Russell Gough

Minimum required scores on the SAT are unfair to minority athletes, Russell Gough argues in the following viewpoint. Gough contends that athletes who have solid academic records in high school should not be penalized because of a poor score on one standardized test. He also asserts that many athletes who do not fulfill the requirement would graduate from college if given the opportunity. Gough is a professor of philosophy and ethics at Pepperdine University in Malibu, California, and the author of *Character Is Everything: Promoting Ethical Excellence in Sports.*

As you read, consider the following questions:

1. What were some of Tai Kwan Cureton's accomplishments in high school, as stated by Gough?
2. According to the author, why did the Educational Testing Service not want SAT scores included in eligibility standards?
3. In Gough's opinion, what is the real hypocrisy in college athletics?

Reprinted from Russell Gough, "Jumping Through Hoops," *Los Angeles Times*, January 15, 1997, by permission. Copyright ©1997 The Times Mirror Company.

A gainst David-vs.-Goliath odds and in the name of hundreds of black student athletes like themselves nationwide, two courageous 18-year-olds from Philadelphia sued the National Collegiate Athletic Association (NCAA) in January 1997 for denying them a sporting chance to make their collegiate dreams come true. The young plaintiffs' class action suit, *Cureton vs. NCAA*, charges that the NCAA's freshman eligibility rules discriminate against black student athletes.

TAI KWAN CURETON'S ACHIEVEMENTS

The allegation is correct and the NCAA's own research proves it.

Throughout his high school career as a track-and-field athlete, Tai Kwan Cureton, one of the plaintiffs, dreamed of "running with the best of 'em" at the collegiate level. And his was no pipe dream, given that several top NCAA schools such as the University of Pittsburgh, Pennsylvania State University, Boston College and the Naval Academy had begun courting Cureton in his sophomore year.

Indeed, Cureton became increasingly attractive to these universities because he proved himself to be not only swift of foot but strong in mind and character as well: an honor roll student for 2½ years, an athlete for three years, president of the student government and president of his school's peer-mediation services—all while working more than 30 hours a week at a local fast-food restaurant.

But despite such an outstanding educational record, the scholarship offers from premier universities vanished abruptly, as did Cureton's hopes of competing against elite track-and-field athletes, all because he did not meet the NCAA's minimum requirement of a 700 score out of 1,600 on the SAT. [The requirement has since been set at 820.]

THE SAT POLICY IS NONSENSICAL

Student athletes who don't make the grade on the SAT are ineligible to compete or receive athletic scholarships during freshman year at top-ranked NCAA schools.

It wouldn't have mattered if Cureton had held a 4.0 grade point average at the nation's top high school. Four years of hard work and verifiable accomplishment in high school are negated by a 3½ hour, multiple choice test. This policy defies common sense.

It also defies basic standards of fairness by discriminating against large numbers of minority students like Cureton. In the early 1980s the Educational Testing Service, which develops and administers the SAT, as well as nonprofit educational groups such as the Boston-based Center for Fair and Open Testing, asked the NCAA not to include SAT scores in its eligibility standards because the scores would have a disproportionately negative impact on minorities and might undermine the overall effectiveness of the effort to raise standards for athletes.

SAT SCORES DO NOT DETERMINE COLLEGE ACADEMIC PERFORMANCE

With success several institutions have dropped the use of standardized tests in their admissions decisions. In *The Case against the SAT*, the authors cite cases where the SAT was optional at Bates and Bowdoin colleges. They also cite the dropping of standardized admissions tests at Harvard Business School and Johns Hopkins Medical School. Both Bates and Bowdoin studied the academic performance of students after the optional use of the exam and found no negative impact. According to Paul Shaffner, a psychology professor at Bowdoin who analyzed his institution's results:

> The feasibility of the policy has been demonstrated. Administrative aspects have worked smoothly; virtually all matriculants were aware of the option to submit or withhold their SAT scores and knew their scores in advance so as to have been able to make informed choices. . . . The policy was overwhelmingly endorsed by students. More important than administrative considerations, though, is that virtually all students in both groups have proved capable of meeting the college's educational requirements. Of the dozen students permanently dismissed for academic and/or disciplinary reasons in the four academic years since fall 1979, only two had withheld SAT scores upon application.

Kenneth L. Shropshire, *In Black and White: Race and Sports in America*, 1996.

In its own study of student athletes admitted before the SAT requirement went into effect, the NCAA found that the rule would have rejected nearly half of all black student athletes who, in fact, went on to graduate from college.

MINORITIES ARE KEPT OUT OF COLLEGE

The NCAA itself proved that its policy was—and is—verifiably locking out hundreds, if not thousands, of qualified minority students from the best NCAA schools.

NCAA leaders defend the policy, saying the latest research shows that graduation rates for black athletes have increased slightly in the past few years. This is true but very much besides the critical point: Large numbers of qualified minority students, like Tai Kwan Cureton, are being discriminated against.

Most disturbing is the way in which the NCAA has very effectively—if even unintentionally—made scapegoats of so-called "dumb jocks" in the name of restoring academic integrity to college sports. While academically unqualified high school seniors have undoubtedly been recruited and exploited in the past by NCAA athletic programs, the foremost problem undermining the integrity of college sports does not involve unqualified recruits. On the contrary, the problem involves colleges and universities uncommitted to seeing their recruits succeed academically.

In terms of time and energy spent, big-time college athletic programs all too often expect much more of their student athletes athletically than academically. Therein lies the real exploitation and hypocrisy: institutions of higher learning making scapegoats of impressionable and vulnerable 18-year-olds to cover up their own lack of educational and ethical resolve.

VIEWPOINT

"The National Collegiate Athletic
Association's [NCAA] leaders ...
don't think their minimum test
scores are all that hard to make. And
they aren't."

COLLEGE ENTRANCE REQUIREMENTS FOR ATHLETES ARE NOT UNFAIR

Tom Knott

In the following viewpoint, Tom Knott contends that minimum
test score requirements for college-bound athletes are not unfair
and serve the necessary purpose of discriminating between
people of varying levels of intelligence. He argues that the scores
are not difficult to achieve and are relevant because grades are
not an accurate indicator of scholastic success since not all high
schools are academically equal. Knott is a columnist and sportswriter for the *Washington Times*.

As you read, consider the following questions:

1. How are "dummy" athletes like idiot savants, in the author's
   opinion?
2. According to Knott, why do few athletes flunk out of college?
3. In Knott's view, what should the NCAA ask the media and
   trial lawyers to overlook if entrance requirements are
   eliminated?

Reprinted from Tom Knott, "Lawyers Are Trying to Make It Easier for Dummies to
Get into College," *The Washington Times*, January 26, 1997, p. 27, by permission of *The
Washington Times*.

A District of Columbia–based, public-interest law firm is trying to level the academic field for minority athletes.

The firm has a problem with the National Collegiate Athletic
Association (NCAA) demand that incoming athletes meet either
the SAT or ACT requirement to play as freshmen. The firm says
the tests are culturally and racially biased.

So these lawyers, the so-called Trial Lawyers for Public Justice,
have done what lawyers do. They have filed a class-action suit
in U.S. District Court in Philadelphia, saying the NCAA's
standardized-test requirement is racially discriminatory.

INTELLECTUAL DISCRIMINATION

You can argue, as people have done for years, about whether the
tests are racially discriminatory. But there can be no argument
about whether the tests are discriminatory. They are. The tests
separate the smart from the dumb.

To be honest, standards, even minimum ones, are discriminatory. There are always going to be those dummies who can't
meet the standards, no matter how easy you make it for them.
There are those dummies who couldn't spell cat if you spotted
them the first two letters, as it once was said of Terry Bradshaw.

People generally don't get too worked up about your basic
dummy. Americans discriminate against dummies all the time.
It's not right. In fact, it's sad, so sad, three-hanky sad. But
people, even the Trial Lawyers, do this all the time. The Trial
Lawyers probably do not have a dummy in their firm, not even a
token dummy. It just wouldn't be smart business, having a token
dummy on the payroll.

But people do care about the dummies who can jump out of
a gym or slip tackles. They are almost like idiot savants. They
might not be able to read and write all that well, but they have
one extraordinary skill. And they have a right to utilize that skill,
even if two-syllable words turn their brains to mush.

COLLEGE ATHLETES DO NOT FLUNK OUT

The NCAA's leaders are in a tough situation. They don't think
their minimum test scores are all that hard to make. And they
aren't. Your basic pet rock could come close to achieving the
minimum score on either the SAT or ACT. You're not dealing
with pet rocks, however. You're dealing with real human beings.

And once these real human beings get into an institution of
higher learning, they do fine. You rarely hear about a big-time
athlete flunking out of college. That's because athletes can take

all kinds of challenging courses to maintain their eligibility. They can take good old remedial English and see Spot run. They can take horseback riding or walking. Or they can live in the P.E. building and do the badminton thing. Or they can do what National Basketball Association (NBA) gynecologist J.R. Rider did and take understanding and preventing premenstrual syndrome. They get all the tutoring they want, and they actually get to know their academic advisor on a first-name basis. They may never get close to graduating, but that's not the point.

ATHLETES SHOULD NOT RECEIVE SPECIAL PRIVILEGES

I am not an athlete, and I don't think the 820 SAT score standard for athletes should be lowered.

If colleges are willing to lower the SAT score for athletes, I think that they should also lower scores for other students who contributed to their schools by spending time with clubs and organizations.

The ticket to making it in the world is to work hard, not to have a free ride. Athletes want to get privileges while other students work hard and are overlooked. Athletes should not put their hearts and souls into sports at the exclusion of studying.

Sandra Lopez, *Los Angeles Times*, June 20, 1998.

The NCAA likes the standardized tests in part, because grade-point averages from high school are sometimes highly misleading. Not all 3.0 grade-point averages are equal. A 3.0 grade-point average at certain high schools may only mean that an athlete did not drool in class.

Anyway, the Trial Lawyers see an injustice, and they are doing all they can to rectify it, as well they should.

The SAT and ACT are merely crutches for the NCAA to show that it is trying to do its job. As it is, athletes just one step up from a pet rock are admitted into all kinds of prestigious universities. Some wind up taking the SAT or ACT test a zillion times before making the mark.

REFORMERS SHOULD NOT COMPLAIN

The NCAA might as well open the door all the way. It wouldn't hurt. It wouldn't make the system less fraudulent. Fraudulent is fraudulent.

If the NCAA waived all requirements, however, the governing body should ask the Trial Lawyers, as well as the media, for some assurances.

They are the following: Don't talk about the graduation rates of student-athletes. Don't be outraged by the thuggery of student-athletes. Don't whine about how student-athletes are exploited.

And remember: You can't have it both ways. You can't champion reforms in college sport but then claim the reforms are discriminatory.

Reforms are intended to be discriminatory, you dummy. Knock-knock.

"Universities should focus on educating students, not on limiting the economic opportunities of their athletes."

COLLEGE ATHLETES SHOULD BE PAID

Dick DeVenzio

In the following viewpoint, Dick DeVenzio argues that the National Collegiate Athletic Association (NCAA) should not bar college athletes from taking payment for participation in their sports. DeVenzio asserts that there is no valid reason why these athletes should not be paid, and he contends that the existing NCAA policy limits college athletes' economic opportunities. DeVenzio is an author and a former high school and college basketball player.

As you read, consider the following questions:

1. According to DeVenzio, why is it strange to make student-athletes sign statements that they are involved in college sports as an avocation?
2. In DeVenzio's view, why should athletes in non-revenue-producing sports not receive the same benefits as athletes in revenue-producing sports?
3. What was Martin Luther King Jr.'s litmus test for the morality of laws, as stated by the author?

Reprinted from Dick DeVenzio's testimony on stipends for student athletes before the House Subcommittee on Commerce, Consumer Protection, and Competitiveness, of the Committee on Energy and Commerce, July 28, 1994.

The National Collegiate Athletic Association (NCAA), each year, is systematically depriving thousands of athletes (and their families) of the opportunity to receive just economic rewards in exchange for their highly valued and coveted talents in football and basketball.

There is no crucial purpose for this deprivation. But rules have become more stringent as the financial value of college basketball and football has grown explosively and (not coincidentally, I think) as the racial makeup of the recruited athletes has become more Black.

No Good Explanations

I don't think the major universities and the NCAA have any excuse for this systematic deprivation except the claim that "we didn't get paid when we played, so why should they?"

All the typical reasons for requiring that athletes remain penniless in the universities' multi-million dollar basketball and football enterprises are suspect:

• They are getting an education. (Most recruited basketball and football players in Division I are unable to take advantage of the education being offered. Less than 30% manage to get diplomas.)

• A scholarship is pay enough. (Who ordained university administrators as the Grand Deciders of how much is enough?)

• They are amateurs. (How so? And why? Is amateurism morally superior to professionalism?)

There is no crucial reason that athletes at major universities should not receive the benefits commensurate with their talents. But NCAA rules prevent athletes from using their popularity and personal initiative to maximize their value.

Universities should focus on educating students, not on limiting the economic opportunities of their athletes.

The NCAA manual claims that students must participate in sports for social, physical and recreational benefits—as an *avocation*. Why force athletes to sign statements to this effect when everyone knows that many athletes (and their coaches) are in this enterprise at a level far beyond "avocation"? Why can't the NCAA acknowledge openly that many athletes view their sport as their primary interest in life? And why can't these athletes pursue their interests with an equal intensity? Should ALL athletes be limited to 20 hours a week of practice? If so, why don't universities limit Chemistry students to 20 hours per week of research? Universities already support three divisions which permit various levels of competition. Why not openly acknowledge that, at the top levels, the competition is more than a hobby for those participants?

The NCAA Does Not Acknowledge Diversity

Universities generally are proud of the diversity of their student bodies. So, why is there such an effort made by the NCAA to make sure that athletes are "like regular students." What regular students are they talking about when they use that phrase? Statistics show that over half the college students in America are over 25 years of age and that nearly half the students in America are part-time students. Why isn't part-time status available to NCAA athletes?

Why must all NCAA athletes fit one narrow mold? Why shouldn't the NCAA allow athletes from technical schools, junior colleges, and community colleges to participate in their games? The NCAA should be trying to accommodate the variety of needs of its prospective student-athletes the way the universities are trying to do for students in general. Why should NCAA competition be only for students in four (or five) year, degree-granting programs? If the NCAA and the universities were truly trying to meet the needs of student-athletes, they would offer broader opportunities instead of trying to make every athlete fit one narrow mold.

Equal opportunity does not require equal treatment. It is ludicrous to require that athletes in non revenue-producing sports get the same benefits as athletes in revenue-producing sports. It is not economically feasible for non-revenue sports teams to travel from Seattle to Tucson or from Chestnut Hill to Miami. Neither tax payers nor football players should be forced to pay for travel expenses of non revenue-producing athletes when those athletes can easily play games with just as much social, recreational and competitive value within 200 miles of home.

The NCAA exploits basketball and football players. It appears to be the intent of the major universities to continue to try to get as much money as possible from basketball and football in order to pay for all of the other sports and their ever-growing sports bureaucracies. There ought to be at least a plan to wean the other sports from dependence on basketball and football revenue. Currently, this is not even an issue being considered.

The NCAA also curtails the so-called "minor sports" and limits the opportunities of minor sport athletes. Few efforts are being made to insure that other sports have the chance of growing into self-sustaining programs—and more popular programs— the way basketball and football have. Currently, these other sports are actually suffering from the cycle of welfare-dependence as a result of the subsidies they get from basketball and football. They are not being permitted to grow, nor are they being permitted to promote themselves in order to become self-sustaining.

GIVE ATHLETES TRUST FUNDS

What crucial purpose is being served by keeping athletes penniless? There is no convincing proof that amateurism is morally superior to professionalism. What negatives would occur if athletes were permitted to receive money from Nike or Chevrolet or any other commercial enterprise—the way coaches can now? What if trust funds, not actual cash, were permitted athletes? This would obviously benefit athletes and their families tremendously. Why is this not allowed? What terrible thing would happen if athletes were permitted to benefit financially from their special talents and popularity? Trust funds linked to educational achievement would obviously encourage more athletes to get diplomas; and there are no known negatives.

The NCAA should not be permitted to continue to make rules which deprive athletes of enjoying the economic opportunities that come along with excellence in a popular American sport.

PROFESSIONALIZE COLLEGE SPORTS

Let's say it straight out: Division I basketball and football are the true minor leagues for the National Basketball Association (NBA) and National Football League (NFL). If our colleges want to field first-rate athletic teams, let them do it the way we do everything else in America: by paying for them. Let's professionalize college sports, up front and cleanly, and end the cynicism, the pretense that any more than 10 percent to 20 percent of top-flight college athletes are genuine students.

Warren Goldstein, *Washington Post National Weekly Edition*, September 23–29, 1996.

The NCAA mission—to provide exercise, competition and social benefits through sports—is accomplished fully through Division III sports. So what justification is there for entering in multi-million dollar TV contracts which force athletes to miss classes in order to accommodate TV schedules? There isn't anything wrong with games of this nature. What is wrong is that the NCAA persists in making a set of claims about the purpose of sports and then goes out and gets involved in contracts that have very different purposes.

Martin Luther King, Jr., in his famous letter to clergymen from Birmingham jail in 1963, defined clearly the litmus test for determining the morality of rules and laws and he explained clearly why some rules should be obeyed and others disobeyed. He cited two simple criteria: (1) did you have a vote in making the law or rule (athletes have no vote within the NCAA) and (2) do the rules or laws apply equally to lawmakers and others subject to the laws. Of course, in the NCAA system, the laws made by the NCAA apply very differently to athletes than to others. Martin Luther King, Jr. would not see any morality in rules that allow coaches and others to benefit from the system—with for example million dollar contracts from Nike—but which do not allow athletes to take advantage of their economic opportunities. Currently, secretaries in many of the big-time sports offices across the nation drive courtesy cars provided by local car dealers, but athletes are not permitted so much as a free ride across campus.

Congress Needs to Help Athletes

By what right, what charter, can state universities limit anyone's economic opportunities? Shouldn't educational institutions stick to educating students instead of limiting their economic opportunities? It seems our institutions of higher learning should be proud of helping their students to maximize their opportunities, not limit them.

The NCAA has shown no willingness nor the ability to make positive reforms on behalf of athletes and their families. The courts have consistently ruled that athletes come under the umbrella or rules of voluntary associations; therefore the athletes have received no justice judicially. And it is very difficult for athletes to help themselves due to the transitory nature of their experience. It is incumbent upon Congress to step in as an advocate on behalf of athletes.

Congressional intervention is particularly important now. In 1989, the NCAA signed a new contract with CBS, raising annual revenue from its basketball tournament from 32 million dollars to 143 million. But since 1989 no basketball players have received any increased benefits. In fact, fewer basketball players get scholarships now than did in 1989. The restrictive rules merely continue to tighten. Now, there is movement in the direction of a football national championship that will bring another new 100 million dollar rise in revenue—and the NCAA will no doubt use that new money also to grow its national sports bureaucracy instead of helping athletes.

Personally, I would ask only that Congress force the NCAA to treat athletes like all other American citizens—able to receive freely offered money and other benefits for their specially valued talents.

"Mandating two years of scholarship for every one year of play would ... prove that college athletics really is about education."

COLLEGE ATHLETES SHOULD RECEIVE SCHOLARSHIP EXTENSIONS

Gregg Easterbrook

In the following viewpoint, Gregg Easterbrook argues that paying college athletes will not improve the quality of education given to many of these students and that offering the athletes additional years on a scholarship would be the better solution. He contends that many of these athletes do not realize until late in their college years that they need an education and could use the extra years to finish their studies. Easterbrook acknowledges that this solution is costly but asserts that it also gives universities the incentive to better educate their athletes. Easterbrook has written for magazines such as the *New Republic*, the *Atlantic Monthly*, and *U.S. News & World Report* and is the author of several books.

As you read, consider the following questions:
1. According to Easterbrook, how do overall graduation rates compare between athletes and nonathletes?
2. How much do football scholarships cost each year at major schools, according to the author?
3. What schools does the author cite as examples of places where football programs and academic achievement are combined successfully?

Every year hundreds of college athletes buy into the dream of a professional sports career. Convinced they will be among the fortunate few to land a lucrative contract, they devote much of their energy and concentration to the practice field, barely sliding by academically in dubious majors like "human potential." Then reality hits. Draft day comes and goes without a phone call. No tryout invitations. The vast majority of hopefuls suddenly face the fact that their dream will never be anything more than that.

ATHLETES WITHOUT EDUCATIONS

By the time this realization dawns, athletes may wake up and finally be ready to apply themselves to their studies. But by then the scholarship money is gone. Big-sports Division I athletes typically receive up to four years of tuition, room, and board. Many universities tacitly allow athletes—especially in football and basketball—to spend those four years on campus while barely cracking a book. The instant their eligibility expires, the former Saturday heroes are abandoned, as schools rush to restock with the next round of dreamers. If all sports (tennis, track, and so on) are included, athletes graduate at a slightly higher rate than college students generally. But for men who play on high-profile Division I football and basketball teams, graduation rates are notably lower than among the student body at large. In these sports, universities keep the considerable revenue that the athlete's talents have generated, while too often the player ends up with no meaningful education.

Because the education of big-sports college athletes is often so poor, it has long been proposed that Division I colleges drop their pretenses and simply pay basketball and football players. But this wouldn't solve the problem. Not only would it spoil amateur athletics but it would still deny many players what they most need to advance in life, an education.

EXTEND THE SCHOLARSHIPS

Consider instead this solution: Change the rules so that for every year a student athlete plays a revenue-producing sport, he receives up to two years of scholarship toward a baccalaureate degree. Students who play major sports and do well academically at the same time—as many do—would graduate on schedule and simply decline the extra years. But for those who frittered away the first four years, the new rule would create a fallback. Once sports eligibility ended and the chagrined 22-year-old awoke to the inevitability that there would be no glamorous pro career with the Chicago Bulls or Pittsburgh Steelers, there would still be up to four years of academic scholarship remaining. The athlete could return to school, hit the books, and get serious about preparing for life.

The National Collegiate Athletic Association (NCAA), which regulates scholarship offers to athletes, could impose such a 2-for-1 regime. Needless to say, universities wouldn't want to pay the high costs of up to eight years of education for each athlete. A big school's current annual cost for football scholarships—typically around $2 million—might as much as double under this plan. But this fiscal hammer would be useful: Its existence would give schools a monetary stake in making athletes take course work seriously from the beginning. Today the NCAA mandates little more than minimal learning for athletes in the major sports. (Basically, anything above failing grades keeps the athlete eligible.) Give universities a financial incentive to really educate players, and no outside pressure would be needed; the schools would motivate themselves. Mandating two years of scholarship for every one year of play would ensure that athletes are no longer treated by their own schools as testosterone-pumped chumps and prove that college athletics really is about education rather than TV fees and gate percentages. This system would help many athletes and penalize only those schools that really aren't bothering to teach their student athletes anyway.

COMBINING ATHLETICS AND ACADEMICS

Education and big-time sports can be combined. Conscientious schools such as Notre Dame and Penn State field exciting and moneymaking football teams, yet also see more than 75 percent of their senior players up on the stage on graduation day, getting degrees. If colleges really care about the education of big-sports athletes, they should keep the halls open to athletes after the pro dream evaporates.

"It's time for athletic department administrators to insist that academics come first."

COLLEGE ATHLETES SHOULD BE ENCOURAGED TO MAKE EDUCATION A PRIORITY

Lisa Nehus Saxon

In the following viewpoint, Lisa Nehus Saxon contends that college athletic department administrators need to emphasize academics over athletics. She asserts that athletic competitions often take precedence over schoolwork, with players missing classes in order to compete. Saxon maintains that colleges should take steps to ensure that athletes who receive scholarships acquire an adequate education, not just a degree, and can be legitimately labeled "student-athletes." Saxon is a sportswriter for the *Riverside Press-Enterprise*.

As you read, consider the following questions:

1. According to a National Collegiate Athletic Association survey, as cited by the author, how many classes did the average student-athlete miss each week?
2. In Saxon's view, what would be one benefit of freshmen athletic ineligibility?
3. How should the term "student-athlete" be used, according to Saxon?

Reprinted from Lisa Nehus Saxon, "College Sports: Time to Insist Athletics Push Academics," *Riverside Press-Enterprise*, September 17, 1996, by permission.

They are called student-athletes. However, in many instances, athlete-students is a more appropriate description. Consider:

GAMES BEGIN EARLIER THAN CLASSES

• At the University of California at Los Angeles (UCLA), running backs Durell Price and Keith Brown may play in as many as three games before ever attending a class. The incoming freshmen made their college football debuts on Sept. 14, 1996, against second-ranked Tennessee. Their college student debuts were to be announced (TBA). UCLA's fall quarter began Sept. 26, the same day the Bruins traveled to Michigan for a Sept. 28 game.

• At the University of Southern California (USC), incoming freshmen reported to campus July 31 to start preparing for the Trojans' Aug. 25 season opener against Penn State in the Kickoff Classic. USC athletic department officials were guaranteed $675,000 for participating in the nationally televised game, and some USC athlete-students paid a hefty price for making themselves available to play. The early start meant many had to quit summer jobs two weeks earlier than usual. That's a lot of potential lost revenue for a college kid.

• At Miami and Rutgers, there were more than 100 students who probably were too tired to concentrate during morning classes on Sept. 13, 1996. The football teams from those schools played Sept. 12, in a nationally televised game.

Miami played The Citadel on Sept. 7, 1996, and Rutgers played Navy.

Do you think players spent more time preparing for that game than any class?

ATHLETICS AND ACADEMICS ARE IMBALANCED

If ESPN wanted to fill a Wednesday-night time slot with college football, how many athletic department administrators would grab a phone?

While college administrators talk a lot about the importance of balancing athletics and academics, it is clear the scales some are using need to be inspected by county government offices of weights and measures. They're badly out of balance.

A National Collegiate Athletic Association (NCAA) survey prepared in 1987–88 revealed that college basketball and football players spent more time on sports than they did preparing for or attending classes—combined. The average athlete-student missed two classes a week.

The NCAA subsequently adopted a rule restricting a student-athlete's participation in a sport to a maximum of 20 hours a week and four hours per day. But there is no way to regulate the amount of time a student voluntarily spends working in the weight room.

ATHLETES SHOULD MEET ACADEMIC STANDARDS

While the acceptance of college largess by academically deficient athletes is perfectly understandable and while blame for their academic infirmities is properly placed on a variety of factors (parental shortfall, poverty, high school indulgence), higher education still has no obligation to smooth their pathway to pro sports—if they are among the rare ones who make it.

Until they prove themselves academically, these so-called victims should not be identified as bona fide college students. They should not receive higher education's most lucrative undergraduate financial aid package plus tax payer–financed government subsidies as officially rationed by the NCAA.

The aim should be to keep these athletes identified as remedial students. Until an individual qualifies, replace him or her with the dispossessed student-athlete who wants to learn and is at least minimally prepared for college. That was the original intent of the 1.600 legislation and Proposition 48 [minimum academic standards for prospective college athletes that have since been revised].

Set the standards and keep them in place! And rejoice that, at least for college student-athletes, we are debating academic standards. The great shame is that the same debate and like standards are not at issue for all undergraduates in a diluted "higher" education system.

Walter Byers with Charles Hammer, *Unsportsmanlike Conduct: Exploiting College Athletes*, 1995.

It's time for athletic department administrators to insist that academics come first. Keeping track of graduation rates is a waste of time, because those numbers reveal how many athletes received a degree, not how many received an education.

SUGGESTIONS FOR ADMINISTRATORS
Instead, administrators should:
• Make scholarship athletes attempt to become scholars by benching those who fail to attend classes and lectures without a good reason.
• Make freshmen ineligible to play during their first academic year, allowing them to compete on the field only after demonstrating an ability to compete in the classroom. (This would benefit student-athletes allowed to enroll in a university despite

falling short of basic academic admissions standards demanded of non-athletes.)

• Make ESPN execs fill that Thursday-night time slot with the best of Lee Corso, or something else.

None of this will happen, of course.

The television revenue produced by sports such as football and basketball is necessary to pay the freight for non-revenue college sports, such as golf, tennis and most women's programs.

And making freshmen ineligible would prompt coaches to demand more scholarships. That means more money, which means it's out of the question, as far as many university presidents and athletic directors are concerned.

THE TRUE MEANING OF "STUDENT-ATHLETE"

However, there is one change that can be made that won't affect the bottom line.

Please use the title student-athlete more judiciously. Reserve it for athletes who are serious students, for those who had the SAT scores and high-school grade-point averages to qualify under general university admissions standards.

Call the others athlete-students. Then encourage them to earn the title student-athlete. And a degree.

"Basketball players shouldn't be forced to go to college."

ATHLETES SHOULD NOT BE OBLIGATED TO MAKE EDUCATION A PRIORITY

John Feinstein

A college education should not be a requirement for basketball players, John Feinstein argues in the following viewpoint. Feinstein contends that, while the National Collegiate Athletic Association (NCAA) should ensure that prospective college athletes do not cheat on their college entrance exams, the National Basketball Association (NBA) should establish a developmental league for those athletes who do not want to enter college immediately after high school. He asserts that such a program would offer athletes the option to enter college later in life, if they so choose, or play in other basketball leagues if they do not become NBA players. Feinstein has written several books on sports.

As you read, consider the following questions:
1. Why do colleges now have to recruit star athletes more frequently than in the past, according to Feinstein?
2. According to statistics cited by the author, what was the average graduation rate for Division I basketball schools?
3. In Feinstein's view, how would the developmental league affect the college game?

Reprinted from John Feinstein, "Not Every Athlete Needs to Go to College," USA Today, November 13, 1997, p. 15A, by permission of the author.

On the eve of the 1997–98 college basketball season, fans of the game have a number of mind-jarring questions to deal with:

- Can Arizona, with all five starters returning, repeat as national champion in March 1998?
- Can North Carolina continue to be a dominant force now that the legendary Dean Smith has stepped down after 36 seasons and a record-breaking 879 victories?
- Will life go on at Kentucky without another legend (at least in his own mind) Rick Pitino, who took millions of dollars from the Boston Celtics to return to the pro game?

CRISES IN COLLEGE BASKETBALL

Of course, those questions are fun, the kind people like to sit around and argue about while they watch ball games, play a round of golf or eat dinner. But there are far more troubling questions facing college basketball, ones that aren't likely to be answered between now and March 30, 1998, when a new national champion will be crowned in San Antonio.

Because the fact is, no matter how glittering and glamorous the game might seem on those romantic winter nights when thousands pack an arena and fill it with noise for two hours, college basketball is a sport on a collision course with a major crisis.

The crisis will not be caused, as so many people think, by players skipping college to go directly to the National Basketball Association (NBA). Four high schoolers turning pro in three years hardly constitutes a major trend. And it won't even be caused by the escalating number of underclassmen leaving college early to turn pro. Those are certainly problems, but they are nothing compared to the whispered about but rarely discussed in public tidal wave that threatens the sport's future: fraud.

ACADEMIC FRAUD IS A PROBLEM

You see, although a majority of the roughly 3,600 young men playing college basketball on scholarship this winter may be legitimate student-athletes, that quaint term the National Collegiate Athletic Association (NCAA) likes to stick on them like a Red Badge of Courage, there is a sizable and important minority that is not. Many of them are the stars who will light up The Final Four in March. A large number of them play for the schools that are ranked in the polls published each week throughout the season.

If you follow college basketball, you hear their stories all the time. Many will attend three or four high schools, looking for one where they can somehow get the grades and core courses required by the NCAA to make them eligible to play. They will also take the standardized tests over and over, seeking that magic number—820, up from 700 in early 1995, on the SAT or 17 on the ACT that will allow them to play. Miraculously, almost all star players end up qualifying. Then they somehow stay academically eligible throughout their college careers, and when they leave stories begin circulating about the fact that they were never seen in class. In other words, they are athlete-athletes, not student-athletes.

Cheating is not brand-new, by any means. But what makes the issue especially pressing this season is that as the NCAA has raised its academic standards for entering freshmen athletes—most recently in 1995—more and more colleges must strain even harder to try whatever they can do to get an athlete into their schools. And the stakes are higher. Unlike in past years, when student-athletes often stayed the full four years, increasingly athletes are turning pro after one or two years, forcing colleges to recruit stars more often.

And although graduation rate statistics can be deceiving, it certainly doesn't speak well for a sport when three of the four teams in the 1997 Final Four (Minnesota, Arizona and Kentucky) had graduation rates for their basketball teams of under 35%. And those teams are not the exception; they are much closer to the rule. North Carolina, the other finalist, had a graduation rate of 85%, but the overall average for all Division I schools was 45%—nothing to write home about.

Two Proposals for the NCAA

What then should be done? To begin with, the NCAA should crack down on athletes shopping for schools and test scores. It shouldn't be that difficult. Insist that anyone applying for an NCAA scholarship take the standardized tests at certain times and certain places with NCAA-paid proctors at the testing sites. Give the test 100 times a year or 200 times a year—you pick a number—but make it as difficult as possible to cheat. Then, pass a rule that anyone who changes high schools as a senior must sit out his or her freshman year of college. A few youngsters may have legitimate reasons for a move, and they should be allowed to petition for a waiver. The majority will not.

Step 2 is far more complicated but just as important. Basketball players shouldn't be forced to go to college, and they shouldn't be force-fed to the NBA at 18, either. The compromise is a developmental league funded by the NBA. If Commissioner David Stern can pour millions into a league for women, he should be able to come up with some money to protect the game's future. The league should consist of eight to 10 teams with 10 players each. Pay everyone between $75,000 and $100,000 a year and make them put $20,000 of that into a trust fund. The schedule should include no more than 40 games—so players aren't going from 25 games a season in high school to 100 in the pros—and as little travel as possible.

ESTABLISH PREPROFESSIONAL PROGRAMS

The competitive athletics program is, essentially, a preprofessional industry, run completely separate from mainstream university endeavors.

Because this high degree of competitive sports activity is antithetical to the goals and ambitions of higher education, it ought to be eliminated.

In its place, professional football and basketball team owners ought to be made to follow the example of baseball and establish an independent, preprofessional, for-profit farm team training program.

Cecil Lytle, *San Diego Union-Tribune*, February 1, 1995.

Players can play up to four years. If, after four years, they aren't good enough for the NBA, they can decide what to do next with their lives: keep playing in other minor leagues or overseas, or take the $80,000 (plus interest) now in their trust fund and go to college—not to play ball but to go to class. By then, college may not seem like such a bad idea.

INCREASED OPTIONS FOR ATHLETES

Similar options are available to students who choose not to go to college—or can't qualify. In 1994, President Bill Clinton's school-to-work proposal became law, which encouraged schools to create more courses to ease students' transition into the workplace. In 1996, the president's Hope Scholarships plan provided tax credits to cover tuition for the first two years of college, as well as for trade schools. Programs such as these are making other options available to noncollege-bound students so that they get the skills that will make them contributing members of society. The same should go for athletes.

Would such a league mean that a number of great players will never play college basketball? Yes. But nowadays many great players are only hanging around for a year or two anyway. This way, those who choose college will do so because they want to and are likely to stay four years and perhaps even graduate. The college game will still be competitive and exciting, perhaps just a little less spectacular.

But it will also be something it isn't right now: real. Right now, many of the best college teams aren't represented by college students. It's well past time to change that.

PERIODICAL BIBLIOGRAPHY

The following articles have been selected to supplement the diverse views presented in this chapter. Addresses are provided for periodicals not indexed in the *Readers' Guide to Periodical Literature*, the *Alternative Press Index*, the *Social Sciences Index*, or the *Index to Legal Periodicals and Books*.

Mark Asher	"The University of Nike-Reebok," *Washington Post National Weekly Edition*, November 27–December 3, 1995. Available from 1150 15th St. NW, Washington, DC 20071.
Lee C. Bollinger and Tom Goss	"Cleaning Up College Basketball," *New York Times*, September 5, 1998.
Bryan Burwell	"NCAA Gets What Richly It Deserves," *Street & Smith's SportsBusiness Journal*, May 11–17, 1998. Available from 120 W. Morehead St., Suite 310, Charlotte, NC 28202.
D. Stanley Eitzen	"Big-Time College Sports: Contradictions, Crises, and Consequences," *Vital Speeches of the Day*, December 1, 1997.
Ken Hamblin	"The Exploitation of Black Athletes," *Conservative Chronicle*, February 5, 1997. Available from PO Box 29, Hampton, IA 50441.
Issues and Controversies On File	"Student-Athlete Compensation," March 20, 1998. Available from Facts On File News Services, 11 Penn Plaza, New York, NY 10001-2006.
John Leo	"Should Stars Get Dunked?" *U.S. News & World Report*, July 17, 1995.
Betsy Peoples	"Colleges Fumble at Graduating Black Athletes: Time Out," *Emerge*, October 1996. Available from One BET Plaza, 1900 W. Place NE, Washington, DC 20018-1211.
Betsy Peoples	"Nothing But Fouls," *Emerge*, March 1998.
Rick Reilly	"The Life of Reilly: The NCAA Has Done a Job on Itself," *Sports Illustrated*, May 4, 1998.
Woody West	"Stain of Recruitment Sleaze Spreads Across Campuses," *Insight*, July 31, 1995. Available from 3600 New York Ave. NE, Washington, DC 20002.
Thad Williamson	"Bad as They Wanna Be," *Nation*, August 10–17, 1998.
Steve Wulf	"Tote That Ball, Lift That Revenue," *Time*, October 21, 1996.

CHAPTER 3

Is Racial Discrimination a Problem in Sports?

CHAPTER PREFACE

On December 1, 1997, during practice, the Golden State Warriors' Latrell Sprewell reportedly threatened to kill his coach, P.J. Carlesimo. Sprewell attacked Carlesimo twice during that practice. Shortly thereafter, the National Basketball Association (NBA) suspended Sprewell for one year, and the Warriors terminated his contract. (In March 1998, an arbitrator reduced the length of the suspension and ordered that the Warriors reinstate Sprewell's contract.)

Although some observers considered Sprewell's behavior and subsequent punishment to be another example of athletes misbehaving, others viewed it as a race-related issue—in particular, the relationships between a black athlete, his white coach, and a league dominated by white owners and management. When Sprewell initially explained what had happened, he contended Carlesimo's verbal abuse led to the incident. Sprewell's agent, Arn Tellem, suggested that Carlesimo's yelling may have had racist overtones and noted that other black players had had disputes with Carlesimo. Tellem also argued that the punishment would have been less severe had Sprewell been white. Monica Moorehead, a political activist and unionizer, supports this view in *Workers World*: "What happened to Latrell Sprewell cannot be viewed within a vacuum. The NBA, like all other institutions in the United States, is riddled with racism and class bias." In addition, San Francisco Mayor Willie Brown and Oakland Mayor Elihu Harris requested that the National Association for the Advancement of Colored People (NAACP) and other civil right advocates investigate the events.

Other critics maintained that race was not a factor in Sprewell's troubles with Carlesimo or the athlete's punishment; rather, they maintained that the violence of the assaults justified the severe penalties. Tim Sullivan, a columnist for the *Cincinnati Enquirer*, comments, "Lord knows the sports world is a long way from colorblind, but some problems run deeper than skin depth. Respect for authority is in decline across racial boundaries." The Reverend Jesse Jackson, a noted advocate of black civil rights, also argued that, while Sprewell's initial punishment was excessive, the suspension and termination were not racist decisions. Some of these analysts acknowledged Carlesimo is known for yelling at his athletes, but they contended that racism did not cause the player-coach dispute.

The treatment of minority athletes, particularly African Americans, has been an issue in sports for decades. In the following chapter, the authors debate whether racial discrimination is a problem in sports.

| "Coaches, like administrators in front
offices, make decisions, either consciously or subconsciously, as to who
plays certain positions based on race."

RACIAL INEQUALITY IN SPORTS IS A SERIOUS PROBLEM

Northeastern University's Center for the Study of Sport in Society

Northeastern University's Center for the Study of Sport in Society is an organization that addresses the problems in sports and shows how sports can help benefit society. The following viewpoint is excerpted from the center's 1997 Racial Report Card, which analyzes the racial composition of players and staff in professional football, baseball, and basketball. The report notes a downturn in minority representation in some sports, and further contends that minority players do not always receive equal opportunities in the sports they play. According to the center's findings, African-American players may be victims of positional segregation since they are more likely to play positions such as running back or outfielder rather than quarterback or pitcher. Furthermore, the center argues that minorities have not been given adequate opportunities to serve as coaches or managers.

As you read, consider the following questions:

1. What was unusual about the Los Angeles Dodgers during the 1997 baseball season, according to the Center?
2. According to the article, how many National Basketball Association (NBA) coaches were African American at the time the report was written?
3. What mental traits do baseball managers believe are necessary for pitching and catching, as stated by the Center?

Excerpted from the 1997 *Racial Report Card* of Northeastern University's Center for the Study of Sport in Society. Reprinted with permission. The entire document is available at the Center's website: www.sportinsociety.org. Orders for this edition and future editions can be placed by contacting the Center at (617) 373-4025.

ny that race plays
shifted, The 1995
become almost en-
ue" for all positions
Racial Report Card
s once again suggest

LEAGUE BASEBALL

	rs	% of Latino Players			
	'83	'97	'96	'93	'83
	7	20	17	12	7
	0	24	25	12	7
19	38	12	9	11	7
13	21	39	37	26	14
12	5	22	17	12	13
8	11	44	43	50	9
50	46	21	18	17	9

1997 Racial Report Card.

Card shows, stacking is again a se-
Major League Baseball. The data
es, like administrators in front of-
consciously or subconsciously, as to
s based on race. Some positions rely
such as speed and reactive time than
g and leadership ability. In the NFL,
nning back, wide receiver, cornerback,
incidence that in 1997, Blacks held 90,
of those positions respectively? Or that
rterbacks and 72 percent of the centers

seball, the 6 percent of pitchers who were
smaller percentage than in 1983 when it
2 percent of the catchers were Black in
baseball's two central positions, ones that
re intelligence, quick thinking and decision-

notable speed and reactive positions are the
. Fifty-one (51) percent of the outfielders were
positions which Blacks occupied in proportion

Northeastern University's Center for the Study of Sport in
Society has completed its ninth annual Racial Report Card
regarding the racial composition of players, coaches and front
office employees in the National Basketball Association, National
Football League, and Major League Baseball. Gender compar-
isons are also provided where they are relevant. The 1997 Racial
Report Card (RRC) represents the first time that The Center has
included comparative data for college sport.

GREATER COVERAGE

It was a year of expanded coverage of the issue of race due to
1997 being the 50th anniversary of Jackie Robinson breaking
Major League Baseball's color barrier. Special attention was paid
to the issue of race in professional sport in public forums, in the
media and on college campuses. The report was issued just after
the 25th anniversary of the death of Roberto Clemente on December 31, 1997. The explosion of Latino talent in baseball in
1997, especially in the post-season and the World Series, also
lent a special interest to Latinos in sports.

The results showed no significant overall breakthroughs in
any of the categories covered in professional sport. . . .

The 1997 Racial Report Card is especially timely not only in
light of the Robinson and Clemente anniversaries but also because President Bill Clinton has inaugurated a national discussion
of race in America. The Presidential Commission, headed by his-
torian John Hope Franklin, turned to the issue on race and sport
early in 1998. Whatever points are up for criticism in this report,
whatever the shortcomings of sport may be when it comes to
ideals and reality, sport remains the one national plane where
people of color and whites seem to have the greatest opportunity
to set a national example for the rest of the country. . . .

PLAYERS AND PERCENTAGES

Because of its milestones in 1997, it is fitting to start with Major
League Baseball.

Baseball has always been filled with ironies on the issue of race.
As the first sport in the modern era to integrate, it has for decades
had the fewest minority players among the three major sports. At
one point during 1997, the Dodgers, the team that broke the barriers in 1947, did not have a single African-American player on
the team.

League-wide, the percentage of African-American players in
1997 hovered near a two decade low at 17 percent. On the
other hand, the percentage of Latinos in Major League Baseball

has continued its upward climb, rising from 20 percent in 1996 to 23.7 percent in 1997. This dramatic rise represents the biggest increase of Latino players in the 1990s.

Other than the 6 percent rise in the percentage of African-American players in the National Football League (NFL) between 1991 and 1992, this year's increase in Latino players in baseball is sport's biggest single-season swing for minorities playing sport. In 1997, the combined total of African-American and Latino players on Major League rosters increased from 37 to 41 percent, an all-time combined high.

In total percentage of players, the National Basketball Association (NBA) continues to lead the way in pro sport for player opportunities for Blacks. At the outset of the 1996-97 season, 79 percent of NBA players were Black, down slightly from last year's 80 percent. However, it should be noted that the 1996-97 figures marked the second consecutive decrease of Blacks playing in the NBA in the 1990s. It is a trend worth watching.

As the 1997 season opened, 66 percent of the NFL players were Black. This is the second straight year that the percentage of Blacks has decreased in the game. While the proportion of whites remained constant in the NFL, it increased by one percent in the NBA. The difference in the NFL was made up with the increase of Pacific Islanders and Latinos, thus leaving the percentage of minority players in the NFL the same. . . .

INSUFFICIENT COACHING AND MANAGING OPPORTUNITIES

Other than players, head coaches and big league managers hold the most visible positions in pro sports. This has always seemed to be the most logical place for Blacks and Latinos to get jobs. After all, who knows sport better than the athletes who played it? It is natural—although not always true—to believe that a former player could transmit the knowledge and skills accumulated over the course of many years of playing to younger players. Many athletes of all colors and ethnic backgrounds have shared this dream. It is far more likely to become a reality if you are white.

Jackie Robinson had two dreams for sport: increased player opportunities and similar increases for front office and coaching positions. The first dream has been overwhelmingly fulfilled. The latter is overwhelmingly unfulfilled.

At the beginning of the 1997 season, Major League Baseball had Felipe Alou of the Montreal Expos as its only Latino manager, Dusty Baker was with the San Francisco Giants, Cito Gaston led the Toronto Blue Jays, and Don Baylor was with the Colorado Rockies as the sport's three Black managers. As the season ended,

PLAYERS FACE POSITIONAL SE

Whenever it is brought up,
segregation is as hotly discuss
it comes to hiring practices, n
numbers and percentages mean

However, when it comes to
which positions are played by

to their percentage in baseball are the infield positions. Latino players did not seem to fit any pattern of stacking. The Center will continue to monitor this closely as it is clearly an area of concern that there has been so little change over so long a period of time. . . .

COMPARING SPORT TO SOCIETY

The goal in publishing The 1997 Racial Report Card is to help professional—and now college—sport recognize that sport, which is America's most integrated work-place for players, is not much better than society in who it hires in front office and decision-making positions. There is widely acknowledged enlightened leadership on issues of diversity in the league offices of the NBA and the NFL. It also exists within Baseball's Executive Committee and at the top of the National Collegiate Athletic Association (NCAA). Nonetheless, white males control the operations on most franchises and in the colleges.

If we couldn't celebrate more victories for diversity in the year of Jackie's 50th, perhaps sport can commit to refocus so it really can lead the nation to find a better way to serve the principle of equal opportunity for all.

VIEWPOINT

"The opportunity is there for
everyone in baseball."

RACIAL INEQUALITY IN SPORTS IS
NOT A SERIOUS PROBLEM

Wayne M. Barrett

Many critics believe that racial inequality pervades college and
professional sports. In the following viewpoint, Wayne M. Barrett argues that people who claim that racism is a problem in
major league baseball are misguided. He contends that minorities have equal opportunities and African-American baseball
players do not face prejudice. In addition, Barrett opposes hiring
additional black executives solely because of their race, a practice he views as reverse discrimination. Barrett is an associate editor of *USA Today* magazine.

As you read, consider the following questions:

1. In Barrett's opinion, how should Bob Watson have celebrated
   the New York Yankees' 1996 World Series victory?
2. How does the author respond to Gary Sheffield's views on
   racism?
3. According to Barrett, what is not guaranteed by the
   Constitution?

Reprinted from Wayne M. Barrett, "Big League Bigotry Comes Full Circle," *USA Today*
magazine, July 1997, by permission of the Society for the Advancement of Education.

The politically correct police—in this case, black professional athletes and their enablers, the liberal sporting press—are at it again. They blatantly are playing the race card in the wake of the season-long celebration marking the 50th anniversary of Jackie Robinson breaking baseball's color barrier.

AN ABSURD STATEMENT

The height of absurdity on this issue was reached in spring 1997 when a column in *The Sporting News* decried, among other things, that the Dodgers, the team for which Robinson played during his 1947-56 Hall of Fame career, currently only have one native-born black American on their roster. The columnist asked: Wouldn't Jackie be ashamed, and sickened, if he were alive today to see how his old team was behaving?

Besides the fact that the Dodgers have had so many black stars over the years that it would be impossible to even begin listing them all, the Los Angeles roster is chock-full of minorities, including many Latin American blacks. The Dodgers' mound staff isn't known as "The International House of Pitchers" for nothing.

AN OVERRELIANCE ON NUMBERS

Perhaps most infuriating is the obsession with numbers. For instance, it has been cited that, in 1959, American-born blacks represented 17.25% of all major league ballplayers. Today, it's 15.4%. If you're going to play that game, blacks only comprise 10% of the general U.S. population, so they're overrepresented by more than five percent in the big leagues. Seriously, though, the game is open to everyone and critics would be hard-pressed to point to any of the 28 major league rosters and not be able to find plenty of minorities.

Actually, the case of general managers is where the black proponents show their true stripes. No sooner had the New York Yankees won the 1996 World Series than Bob Watson was addressing a post-game press conference saying how proud he was to be the first black GM in history to guide a championship team. Imagine if a white man claimed to be the white embodiment of baseball genius? Couldn't Watson have celebrated the pinnacle of his wonderful career as both a prominent player and ground-breaking general manager on an individual basis, simply expressing happiness and gratitude at finally being part of a World Series champion, which is, after all, the ultimate goal of all baseball personnel? Instead, he had to hold himself up as a symbol of a race, hoping to spur the hiring of other blacks based on his success.

BASEBALL AND CIVIL RIGHTS

Beyond the obvious platitudes, baseball's long struggle over race can yield some surprising perspectives on our national predicament. The Jackie Robinson epic is generally lumped in with the 1954 Brown decision against segregated public schools and the 1964 Civil Rights Act outlawing job discrimination. Yet two crucial differences stand out. 1) The integration of organized baseball *preceded* the civil-rights revolution, and in reality baseball helped make later reforms politically feasible by giving white Americans black heroes with whom to identify. 2) Government had almost nothing to do with this triumph of the competitive market. Baseball owners finally realized that the more they cared about the color of people's money, the less they could afford to care about the color of their skin.

Steve Sailer, *National Review*, April 8, 1996.

The liberal press agreed, bemoaning the fact that there hasn't been a subsequent rush to hire black executives. In other words, if one black man succeeds, then automatically all black GMs will bring their teams success. Yet, isn't that a case of reverse discrimination, hiring someone based on the color of his skin? Well, since Ken Caminiti of the San Diego Padres won the National League Most Valuable Player award, all clubs should look to draft and trade for Italian-Americans. Speaking of Italian-Americans, Joe Torre, who managed the 1996 Yankees, ended a three-decade-plus record of futility of never having won the World Series as either a player or manager. Does this mean that if a club wants to win the World Series, it had better hire an Italian? Or better still, does this mean that Italians make lousy managers because it took Torre so long to win a title? Isn't it ludicrous to attach race labels to individual success or failure?

PREJUDICE DOES NOT EXIST

"People don't want to face the facts; people don't want to hear the truth," Florida Marlins outfielder Gary Sheffield told *The Sporting News*. "But we know what's happening out there. No one's fooling us. I can honestly say racism is worse today than it's ever been in the years I've played. . . . You want to know why there aren't any black players? Because you've got to be twice as good as anyone else. If you're not, you just won't make it. Why do you think you hardly ever see any black bench players? You better be a star, or you're not making this team. They don't want a black player sitting on the bench making money. You got to be white."

Now wait a minute. For starters, Sheffield, Albert Belle of the

Chicago White Sox, and Barry Bonds of the San Francisco Giants—all of whom are black—are three of the surliest and most uncooperative players in baseball today. They also are the three highest-paid players in the game, as each pulls down about $10,000,000 per year, despite never having helped their respective teams into the World Series (never mind winning one). Some prejudice!

As for black bench players, Dodger Manny Mota made a career as a pinch-hitter extraordinaire. Rickey Henderson, at $6,000,000 per annum, is coming off the bench for the Padres. It is true, however, that there aren't a lot of high-salaried black reserves. Then again, there aren't a lot of high-salaried white reserves either. In this age of astronomical salaries, teams empty their bankrolls on their stars and try to save on the reserves. Aging stars used to finish their careers coming off the bench. No longer, unless they're willing to take a big cut in pay. When that deal is offered to blacks, more often than not, they scream racism. Club owners don't need those headaches, so they avoid the situation altogether.

EVERYONE IS GIVEN AN OPPORTUNITY

As for Sheffield's charge that a black must be a premier player to make the team, if what he says is true, that means there are no mediocre blacks in baseball today. A look at the standings and the stat sheet says otherwise, as there is no shortage of so-so players of all races and creeds.

The President of the National League, Leonard Coleman, is black. His predecessor, Bill White, also black, did a miserable job, but that didn't stop the Senior Circuit from going back to the well for its next chief executive. The U.S. Constitution guarantees equality of opportunity, not result. The opportunity is there for everyone in baseball. Screaming racism every time you are passed over for a job, promotion, or pay raise isn't going to get it done. The idea is to keep plugging and stand on your merits as a person and a professional. No one likes a crybaby, especially a bigoted one.

"If Blacks are smart enough to play the game, then they sure as hell have the intelligence to be solid field generals."

MINORITY COACHES FACE DISCRIMINATION IN HIRING

New York Amsterdam News

In the following viewpoint, the New York Amsterdam News contends that the National Football League (NFL) does not offer qualified black assistant coaches the opportunity to become head coaches. The newspaper argues that because black athletes predominate in football, the sport should have more black head coaches. It asserts that teams such as the San Francisco 49ers and St. Louis Rams have unfairly ignored qualified black candidates in order to hire white coaches. The New York Amsterdam News is a weekly newspaper that covers news for the African-American community.

As you read, consider the following questions:

1. Who are three men the newspaper cites as deserving head coaching jobs?
2. According to the New York Amsterdam News, why was the hiring of Dick Vermeil as the head coach of the St. Louis Rams especially troubling?
3. In the newspaper's view, what role should journalists play in ending unfair hiring practices?

Reprinted from "It's Time for the NFL to Give Black Coaches Opportunity," editorial, New York Amsterdam News, March 1, 1997, by permission.

I t's time for the National Football League (NFL) to give Black coaches opportunity.

The NFL head coaching roulette wheel has spun around several times during early 1997 and not once has it landed on black. This is an injustice that must be addressed by team owners and commissioner Paul Tagliabue's office.

THE NFL IGNORES QUALIFIED BLACK CANDIDATES

The National Football League began its 77th season in 1997. There are 30 head coaching positions in a game that Black athletes predominate. Yet only three teams currently have African Americans as their top man: Dennis Green (Minnesota Vikings), Tony Dungy (Tampa Bay Buccaneers), and Ray Rhodes (Philadelphia Eagles).

Eleven franchises have hired new head coaches, including the New York Jets, the New York Giants and the San Francisco 49ers. None of them gave any serious consideration to deserving men like Sherman Lewis, the Green Bay Packers' offensive coordinator, Emmitt Thomas, the Philadelphia Eagles' defensive coordinator, or Art Shell, the erstwhile head coach of the Los Angeles Raiders.

Instead, the "old boys" network called upon some of its retreads to fill the vacancies. Bobby Ross, who coached the San Diego Chargers in 1996, was hired to replace Wayne Fontes in Detroit. Dan Reeves, who has little love for Giants general manager George Young, was selected by Atlanta Falcons ownership to return to his native Georgia and resurrect an abysmal team. In New Orleans, Mike Ditka replaced the fired Jim Mora as the Saints' savior. Ditka's hiring had as much to do with selling tickets as it did with winning ballgames.

Lewis has Super Bowl rings to show for the impeccable job he has done as a member of both the San Francisco 49ers and Green Bay Packers coaching staffs. Mike Holmgren—who before being named Green Bay's coach in 1991 was the offensive coordinator for the 49ers—brought the cerebral Lewis with him from San Francisco to be the Packers' offensive coordinator.

FURTHER INDIGNITIES

San Francisco didn't even have the professional courtesy or decency to wait until after the Super Bowl (it is considered tampering to speak with a coach or even hint at an interest in his services while his team is still playing) to interview Lewis for their opening after parting ways with former coach George Seifert. Instead they plugged the hole with University of California coach Steve Mariucci, another former 49ers assistant who ironically worked under Lewis during his tenure there.

The worst example of Black coaches being ignored in favor of their white counterparts was the hiring of Dick Vermeil to change the fortunes of the St. Louis Rams. Out of football for the better part of two decades, Vermeil, who in his last NFL tour was coach of the Eagles, was working as an analyst for ABC primarily covering college football. He had no business being afforded the chance to become a head coach in the NFL once again before Lewis or Thomas were given their initial opportunity. It is wrong and league executives cannot just sit back and turn a blind eye.

Reprinted by permission of Mike Luckovich and Creators Syndicate.

To date, no official statement has been released by the NFL explaining their position on the subject. But this is an issue that they should not be allowed to trivialize and the matter should be of utmost importance to everyone affiliated with professional football.

EXPLAINING THE INEQUITY

How, in 1997, almost 80 years since the great Fritz Pollard became the first African American to coach a professional football team (Pollard co-coached the Akron Pros to an 8-0-3 finish and the unofficial championship of the American Professional Football Association) has such overt inequity and biasness flourished?

"The 'It's my bat and ball syndrome' persist," said one Black assistant coach. "The owners figure they are in control so therefore they play by their own rules. Unfortunately, we are left on the outside looking in."

Attempts to reach Tagliabue were unsuccessful, as well as the three current Black head coaches and several assistants. When one assistant was contacted his response was: "Do you think I'm going to sit here and address this topic? I'm going to let you writers handle that. It's nothing but negatives. I'm not even going to grace that platform," he said with obvious anger and disappointment resonating with every word.

ELIMINATING RACISM

What can be done to alter this pattern of racism? Black coaching candidates are reluctant to speak out for fear that what little chance they have of landing a head coaching position would be jeopardized. Some may view that approach as selling out or succumbing to the white power structure, which is the furthest assessment from the truth. These proud men have dedicated a lifetime to the sport and would certainly be labeled big mouths, trouble makers and rebellious, and subsequently would never be given a shot.

The established Black veteran players who are well respected around the league must become a powerful voice. The Reggie Whites and Emmitt Smiths and Jerry Rices must make their presence felt. Many of the current players have post-playing aspirations of becoming coaches. If today's athletes do not strongly state their feelings on the lack of opportunities being presented to coaches of color, they will find that doors will be slammed in their faces when they go knocking. A collaborative pioneering effort needs to be put in place immediately.

Journalists both Black and white must fess up to the truth and start exploring the topic more passionately. It is no secret that the media plays a major role in the firing and hiring of coaches. If Blacks are smart enough to play the game, then they sure as hell have the intelligence to be solid field generals. Pressure must be applied on the owners to reverse this disturbing practice.

For the moment, though, it seems as these millionaire, and in some instances billionaire, owners have little intentions of doing the right thing. And the myriad Black assistants can only sit back and watch as the color of their skin is the only reason they are being denied a fair opportunity.

"More important decisions are being made by black men in sports than ever before."

MINORITY COACHES AND OTHER PERSONNEL ARE FACING LESS DISCRIMINATION IN HIRING

Mark Whicker

In the following viewpoint, Mark Whicker argues that, although racism still exists in sports, more and more minorities are attaining positions in front offices and on coaching staffs. He cites a variety of teams and media outlets where an African-American man is in a position of power. Whicker contends that these success stories indicate that minority athletes whose playing careers have ended will be chosen for leadership positions if they stay active within the sport and seize opportunities when they come. Whicker is a sports columnist for the *Orange County Register*.

As you read, consider the following questions:

1. What form of racism exists in the National Collegiate Athletic Association (NCAA), according to Whicker?
2. According to the author, how did Cito Gaston become a major league manager?
3. In Whicker's view, where in society are black men more likely to find racial equality?

Reprinted from Mark Whicker, "Racism Exists, but Playing Field Gets More Level," *Orange County Register*, January 31, 1996, by permission.

While we were arguing and comparing and lamenting the situation, the situation changed.

While we were playing silly scoreboarding games with the progress of black men in sports, the scoreboard moved.

AFRICAN-AMERICAN SUCCESS STORIES

In January 1996, an African-American man is:

The football coach at Oklahoma.

The football coach at Oklahoma State.

The basketball coach at Georgia.

The coach of the Philadelphia Eagles.

The longtime quarterback of the Eagles whom the coach decisively replaced.

The quarterback of the Eagles with whom the coach replaced the longtime quarterback.

The coach of the Tampa Bay Buccaneers.

The chief operating officer of the NCAA.

The basketball coach at Mississippi, only 32 years after James Meredith. [Meredith was the first African-American to attend the University of Mississippi.]

The general manager of the New York Yankees.

The president of the National League.

FURTHER ACCOMPLISHMENTS

The presidents of both National Basketball Association (NBA) expansion franchises, the Raptors and Grizzlies.

The studio host of Fox Sports.

The studio host of NBC's National Football League (NFL) telecasts.

The quarterback of Nebraska, the two-time national football champion.

The quarterback coach of Nebraska.

The manager of the Colorado Rockies, who also was voted Manager of the Year in the National League.

The coach and general manager of the Philadelphia 76ers, at least for a few more months.

The coach and general manager of the Boston Celtics.

The head of public relations for the National Football Conference.

The football coach at Stanford.

The head of the NFL Players Association.

The past two heads of the NBA Players Association.

The studio host for ESPN's "NFL Prime Monday."

One of the two sports anchors at CNN.

Major college basketball coaches in Miami, Memphis, Houston, New Orleans and Atlanta.

The head coach of the Buffalo Bills, for a few weeks while Marv Levy recuperated.

The New Year's Day quarterbacks at Syracuse, Clemson, and Penn State—not to mention bowl teams such as Kansas, Michigan State, North Carolina, Texas and East Carolina.

SOME RACISM REMAINS

What does it mean?

Before we draw any conclusions from this list, let's first point out what it doesn't mean.

It doesn't mean sufficient or satisfactory progress, because there is no such thing. There is no quantitative way to gauge the "right" numbers of influential blacks in sports, because the concept of a "right" number is an insult to everyone involved.

It doesn't mean racism is dead in sports, any more than it's dead in America.

There is racism in the fact that the NCAA continues to use the irrelevant SAT and ACT tests to determine an athlete's eligibility.

BLACK COACHING CANDIDATES SHOULD BE PROACTIVE

Too often, black candidates whine about the lack of opportunities and yet they don't seek out those doing the hiring. They stay in the crevices, intimidated by the outside, clumsy with the new setting, unwilling to play the political game. That needs to stop. Black candidates need to break the circle and hop aboard the spinning carousel. They need to quit giving someone a reason not to hire them.

Shaun Powell, *Newsday*, September 28, 1997.

There was probably racism in the reluctance of the NFL to accept Jeff Blake as a quarterback, up to the time in 1995 when he became the NFL's highest-paid player.

There is at least a smidgen of racism every time a commentator or a sports writer refers to a black player's "athleticism" and a white player's "court sense." There will always be racism, as long as there is mankind.

And it doesn't mean that the savage reaction to the addled remarks of Al Campanis, Jimmy The Greek and Marge Schott hasn't paid dividends. The glass offices of the establishment needed to be rattled. An athletic director or a general manager needed to be reminded to stop and think: Wait a minute. Am I leaving somebody out?

HARD WORK IS REWARDED

But what does that long—and incomplete—list mean?

It means there are indeed rewards to working through the system. Bob Watson, general manager of the Yankees, did not demand an easy chair when he finished playing. He went on the road as a scout. Cito Gaston, manager of the two-time world champion Toronto Blue Jays, did not point at Larry Bowa and Bobby Valentine and other white managers who were presented with major league jobs. He worked long hours as a batting instructor. When his chance came, he maximized it.

When the color barrier fell, there was tokenism. Maury Wills was not ready to manage the Seattle Mariners, and he did not manage them long. He was hired for his renown and for his color.

But when Georgia needed a basketball coach last spring, it picked Tubby Smith, who had taken Tulsa to NCAA Tournament Final 16 appearances in '94 and '95, who had learned and grown as a Kentucky assistant coach. The color of his skin was as meaningless as the color of his car would have been.

Has anyone digested what's happening here?

More important decisions are being made by black men in sports than ever before.

So this is not a plea for congratulation.

It is just a recognition that there is one place in America where black men can find something close to a level playing field.

That place is the playing field itself.

> "An awareness of the history of
> struggle in sport is certainly not too
> much to ask of our athletes."

AFRICAN-AMERICAN ATHLETES SHOULD SPEAK OUT AGAINST RACISM

Kenneth L. Shropshire

In the following viewpoint, Kenneth L. Shropshire maintains that African-American athletes must take action and speak out against racism in sports. He contends that if these athletes join in a unified effort, racial inequality will more likely be reduced. However, Shropshire admits, many athletes are apathetic or are vocal only on issues such as individual salaries. Shropshire is the author of several sports books and a professor at the Wharton School at the University of Pennsylvania. This viewpoint was excerpted from his book *In Black and White: Race and Sports in America*.

As you read, consider the following questions:

1. What are some actions a union could take to combat racism, according to the author?
2. Which African-American athletes does Shropshire note as having faced harassment?
3. In the author's view, what is the ill effect of athletes' lack of knowledge concerning sports history?

It's not my place to fight it, that's why we have a Jesse Jackson. I don't agree with discrimination or racism, but I'm not in the front office. I'm on the front line. I'm a black athlete who has been well taken care of.

—Barry Bonds, quoted in *Sports Illustrated*, April 5, 1993 . . .

To combat racism in sports, we must deal with both what America and sports in reality look and act like and the paragon of what they should look and act like in that ideal moment in the future. To get there, an intermediate period of transition is necessary. This transition period may well become permanent. The concept of permanence is not highly regarded by the courts in the current state of antidiscrimination jurisprudence as it relates to affirmative action programs. The law will continue to wrestle with this problem, but currently, to be upheld, the plans must in all likelihood have a termination date in order to pass judicial scrutiny. Alex Johnson has written appropriately:

> My ideal society is one in which race is, during a transition period, viewed and thought of in much the same way as we view religion; at worst, as a matter to be tolerated, at best, as one to be prized as a product of our diversity. In this ideal society, race is taken into account not in awarding entitlements, but as an important characteristic that is acknowledged and that mandates limited differential treatment. This recharacterization of race is accomplished through the adoption of a multichromatic conception of race that respects racial diversity rather than condemning it. Similarly, diversity is viewed as part of society's strength rather than as part of its weakness. It is only through this transitory stage in which diversity is prized or simply tolerated that the ideal society can ultimately be achieved.

How can the sports industry move into this transition phase? . . .

ATHLETES SHOULD TAKE ACTION

The individuals with the most distinctive power, although not direct hiring power, are the athletes themselves. They are the key stakeholders in the sports business. They must take the risk and act. The athlete activists have historically been individuals who transcended sports in their actions. Muhammad Ali's stance against the Vietnam War and Arthur Ashe's battles against apartheid in South Africa and AIDS worldwide are prominent examples. Change will not come about, however, without a unified effort.

The unified effort can be conducted in a wide range of ways. Union activity would probably be the "safest" and most respected route for a combined effort by athletes. Any players union could avoid the problems which an isolated group of athletes face. But even unions have limitations on how far they can go to bring about more appropriate racial representation in sports. Unions or other groups of athletes or teams might threaten to strike all-star games or to boycott the Super Bowl. Progress will not come without risk. African-American athletes might declare a "Black Saturday" to boycott a particular college sport.

POSSIBLE APPROACHES

The use of leverage is a relatively simple, if risky, concept. Some of the actions by athletes would not have to be complex. Imagine the following scenario: A college recruiter is sitting in the home of a highly touted African-American student-athlete. During the discussion the young man says, "Coach, one thing that my parents and I feel is important for me to consider is the number of persons in positions of authority within your athletic department who are African-Americans. It is important to me because it reflects what the university thinks of me as an African-American and gives me some understanding of what my opportunities may be once I finish playing and may wish to coach or become involved in athletic administration."

An even greater opportunity for this type of action exists at the professional level. With free agency in its current state, imagine a highly sought-after free agent who is African-American speaking to the press about the teams he will consider joining. He says, "One thing that is important to me in selecting a team is the number of African-Americans in positions of authority with the team. It is important to me because it helps me define what my opportunities may be with that team after my playing days have ended." The short career of the athlete, as well as the subjectivity that is involved in determining careers, makes it that much more difficult to take the steps that may bring about change. Any action off the field may be cause for reduced playing time on the field, from management's viewpoint.

MANY ATHLETES ARE APATHETIC

The epigraph quoting Barry Bonds at the beginning of this viewpoint indicates the attitude of those athletes who either do not care to follow history or are not aware of it. It is only fair to note that Bonds did make a public statement on discrimination when he believed race had something to do with the smaller salaries he and other black superstars were being paid relative to their white counterparts. Bonds told *Jet* magazine, "Do you think Bobby Bonilla is worth more or less than Andy Van Slyke [a white ballplayer who received a larger contract than Bonds and

Bonilla]? You know why. Let's leave it at that. He's [Van Slyke's] the Great White Hope here."

Bonds and baseball are not alone in addressing inequality only as it pertains to individual matters like salaries and playing time. According to one National Basketball Association (NBA) franchise executive, regarding athletes, "I really don't think they care. I'm not trying to make our players look bad by any means, but they're very self-focused." And athletes are not the only African-Americans failing to step to the plate on overall race issues. Jesse Jackson proclaimed in 1994 that "many of our youth have not won anything. They've not won a boycott. They are not tough political fighters. And now they have a low confidence level."

A LACK OF POLITICAL POWER

At a time when black political power is actually shrinking, there is no political mandate to enhance black representation in any social sector. The sports media, which serve predominantly white audiences, see no advantage in ceding a share of their power to blacks; the black media (and the black middle class they serve) have embraced the abundance of black athletic celebrities as emblems of racial achievement. There is not enough black wealth to purchase controlling ownership in professional teams or major media, and black athletes, like the vast majority of elite athletes around the world, possess neither the interest nor the political sophistication to mount a campaign against the prevailing order of things.

John Hoberman, *Darwin's Athletes: How Sport Has Damaged Black America and Preserved the Myth of Race*, 1997.

One executive placement specialist in the sports business indicated that an additional problem exists:

I'll assist an African-American to get a position, and they are not pro-active in looking to bring other minorities in. There are much fewer pro-actives. The sports world has never been pro-active. It's difficult to get those in power to even meet people. The whole sports world is a good-old-boy network.

Once African-Americans are in positions of power, networking with African-American contacts can only improve the system. An example where this worked was the hiring of Tyrone Willingham, an African-American, as the head football coach at Stanford University. One of his major supporters was Minnesota Vikings and former Stanford head coach Dennis Green, who also happens to be an African-American. No major protest was required, simply participation in existing networks.

There are a few stars of the 1990s, in addition to Bonds, who have taken solo stances on race issues. Baseball player David Justice told a reporter, "There are a lot of good guys on this team, but there are a few who I know use the 'N' word when I'm not around. . . . How many white players do you see get abused in the paper? We see it happen all the time with black players. No matter what you do, you're still a nigger. Baseball is just an extension of life." *Sports Illustrated* reported that one of Justice's black teammates told him, "I'm glad you said that, but I never could have."

Also supportive of this sort of speaking out is the coauthor of the Episcopalian pastoral letter condemning racism, the Reverend Arthur Williams. Williams told National Public Radio:

> African-Americans, as they move ahead in society . . . often will find themselves not speaking clearly and sharply, confronting racism, enjoying the benefits of the system if they can kind of move into that without being noticed. . . . Call people on their racism. Just don't sit back and melt in.

Individuals with the success and income of the superstar athlete have much to lose by being involved in political action. In fact, when they are riding high, they may not receive any of the negative treatment the average African-American in society might encounter. Occasionally a star or former star finds out otherwise. Baseball Hall of Famer Joe Morgan was harassed by police at the Los Angeles International airport, Boston Celtic Dee Brown was stopped and thrown to the ground by Boston police, and National Football League (NFL) star linebacker Bryan Cox of the Miami Dolphins was called racial epithets by Buffalo Bills fans as he entered Rich Stadium in Buffalo.

More Awareness Is Needed

An awareness of the history of struggle in sport is certainly not too much to ask of our athletes. When writer-broadcaster Bryan Burwell was a sports columnist with the *Detroit News*, a quote from a 1991 interview he conducted was cited quite frequently. Burwell was asking a nineteen-year-old African-American Major League Baseball prospect, Eddie Williams, about his plans for the future. Williams was a catcher, so Burwell asked him if he could imagine what it must have been like for Josh Gibson in the Negro Leagues. When Burwell informed Williams that the Hall of Fame catcher was barred from the opportunity Williams was getting, the young catcher responded, "Never have a chance to play in the majors? Wow, I could never imagine that. Never in a million years." This lack of knowledge about past struggles and successes isolates today's athletes from the larger role they play in society.

Whatever the strategy, the goal should be for those who have not historically had the opportunities in the power positions in sports to gain power—that is, to have the opportunity to show they can excel at the task.

| "Black athletes should not be expected to ... shoulder the burden of racial activism."

AFRICAN-AMERICAN ATHLETES SHOULD NOT BE OBLIGATED TO SPEAK OUT AGAINST RACISM

Adolph Reed Jr.

African-American athletes should not be required to speak out on social issues such as racism, argues Adolph Reed Jr. in the following viewpoint. Reed contends that it is racially unjust to expect athletes such as Tiger Woods and Michael Jordan to be politically active when white athletes are allowed to be apolitical. In addition, Reed asserts, this unwarranted expectation parallels the attitudes held by coaches and scouts who believe that African-American athletes should be more physically talented than their white counterparts. Reed is a professor of African-American studies at the University of Illinois at Chicago.

As you read, consider the following questions:
1. According to Reed, what was Tiger Woods expected to do after winning the Masters?
2. Why was labeling Jackie Robinson a spokesman unfair, in Reed's view?
3. According to the author, why were Roberto Clemente and Frank Robinson maligned during their careers?

Reprinted from Adolph Reed Jr., "Black Athletes on Parade," The Progressive, July 1997, by permission of The Progressive, 409 E. Main St., Madison, WI 53703.

It's difficult to be patient with the argument that the crossover popularity of Tiger Woods or Michael Jordan or Bill Cosby or Oprah Winfrey proves that racial injustice has been defeated. That reasoning is either a straight-up rightist canard or a more or less willfully naive, ostrich-like evasion.

Equally frustrating is the "nothing-has-changed-since-slavery" line that seems to have gained currency in black political discourse as the realities of the Jim Crow world slip out of collective memory. Recently I was on a panel with a black political scientist who insisted that things had gotten no better for black people in this country since 1619; I once saw Derek Bell, then a tenured Harvard Law professor, flamboyantly push a version of the same line. This is, of course, a self-discrediting argument. How many black people were on the Harvard Law School faculty or teaching in predominantly white universities thirty years ago, much less earlier?

SPORTS AND RACIAL OBLIGATION

But while there has been undeniable progress, racialized expectations still prevail—especially in sports.

Tiger Woods's Masters victory made him a social spokesman for black athletes. It's a familiar pattern. Woods was not only expected to comment on how his accomplishment, as the first black winner of the most Southern of all Professional Golfers' Association (PGA) tournaments, related to Jackie Robinson; he also was called upon to pay homage to Charlie Sifford, Lee Calvin Peete, Lee Elder, and other black trailblazers on the PGA tour.

Woods's responses seemed reasonable enough and genuine. His acknowledgement that he had paused on the last hole of the last Masters round to reflect that he was walking a path carved by his black predecessors was even affecting.

By contrast, Chicago White Sox star Frank Thomas created a bit of a media stir by admitting that he doesn't know much about Jackie Robinson or his sport's racial history. The ensuing controversy centered on Thomas's—and, by extension, other black athletes'—larger social and racial obligations.

THE IMAGE OF TIGER WOODS

This theme of special obligation also figured into the Tiger Woods hype. All along he has been trumpeted as a "role model" for black—and Asian American—kids. He's a clean-cut, articulate, and apparently earnest young man whose public persona isn't flamboyant or especially controversial. Nike, evoking the concluding scene from Spike Lee's *Malcolm X*, projects Woods as such a role model in an ad that quick-cuts to nonwhite kids all over the globe who proclaim, *seriatim*: "I am Tiger Woods."

Woods now joins Michael Jordan among the company's most visibly promoted human icons. Jordan has been the object of criticism for his silence about Nike's horrible labor practices in its offshore production operations. (The stunning fact is that Nike pays him more than the annual payroll of its entire Indonesian workforce.) He has been criticized as well for not speaking out or being conspicuously active on behalf of black issues and causes. Woods, similarly, has been faulted by some for not being a vocal enough race man—though disclosures of racist threats and harassment he's received on the golf circuit give those objections a strange twist.

The fact that people have such expectations of athletes like Jordan and Woods is Jackie Robinson's ironic legacy. Robinson's stardom as a baseball player was inseparable from his political renown for breaking the color bar in a very visible arena of American culture. His views were solicited on all manner of political and social issues that concerned black Americans.

ROBINSON'S RESPONSIBILITIES

This was understandable, especially at the time: Robinson symbolically represented the goals of the burgeoning civil-rights movement and large social and political aspirations of black Americans much more broadly. At the same time, though, the spokesman status thrust onto him was both unfair to him (though he may not have bristled at it) and deeply troublesome politically. After all, Jackie Robinson had no special expertise for this role. He was a baseball player. Nor was he accountable to any particular body to speak in the name of black Americans.

In addition to carrying the weight of race spokesmanship, Robinson also faced constant scrutiny for deportment. Indeed, he was selected as the pathbreaker partly because of his articulate, All-American demeanor. And his agreement not to retaliate against affronts—no matter how bad—was a precondition of the whole arrangement.

NO HIGHER STANDARDS

In a racially just world, black athletes should not be expected to hold to a higher standard of behavior than whites. Nor should they be expected to shoulder the burden of racial activism. And do we really want the likes of Charles Barkley, the National Basketball Association's (NBA's) most prominent black Republican, or the Philadelphia 76ers' loutish rookie of the year, Allen Iverson, declaiming on social affairs in the name of black Americans?

Sure, it would be good and useful for Michael Jordan and Tiger Woods to exert pressure on Nike to clean up its dreadful labor practices. But the implication that they have some special obligation to do so because of their status as black—or in Woods's case, even Asian American—athletic icons is wrong.

Woods and Jordan have the right to be apolitical no less than Larry Bird, Pete Sampras, Wayne Gretzky, or Brady Anderson. Frank Thomas has the right to have grown up playing baseball without paying much attention to the sport's history, even the history of its desegregation, from which originates his opportunity to become wealthy playing it. When you boil off the self-righteous presumptions about special racial responsibility, Thomas's ignorance about Jackie Robinson is not really different from that of many young players who don't know much about the game's history or stars of the past. Reverence for, or even interest in, a sport's lore isn't a condition for being able to play it well; nor should it be.

ATHLETIC MYTHS STILL EXIST

The presumption that black athletes should shoulder greater social expectations at least bears a family resemblance to the persisting myth of special black athletic prowess, which in turn, works to perpetuate the worst stereotypes and to undermine the careers of black professional athletes in general.

On the average, blacks in pro baseball and football perform somewhat better statistically than their white counterparts. At first glance this fact may seem to lend credence to the claim that blacks are more gifted. The reality, however, is quite the opposite: Marginal black players are more likely than comparably talented whites to get weeded out along the way.

The myth of black athletic superiority leads scouts and coaches to evaluate black athletes with higher expectations in mind. So the black player needs to exhibit a higher level of skill or performance to impress.

Black athletes who don't perform up to inflated expectations are more likely to be characterized as lazy, malingering, or otherwise possessed of bad attitudes. In 1980, for example, Houston Astros' star pitcher J.R. Richard nearly died when he suffered a career-ending stroke on the field. He had been complaining of weakness for some time, but when no clear medical basis for his complaint was detected right away, the reaction of the Astros' management and the Houston media was to attack Richard for dogging it, even though Richard had been among the league's leaders in innings pitched for several years. After he collapsed, a medical exam disclosed a blood clot. Earlier treatment would probably have saved his career as the most dominating pitcher in baseball.

ATHLETES SHOULD BE TREATED EQUALLY

Frank Robinson and Roberto Clemente have been enshrined on the highest echelon of Major League's pantheon of heroes, and rightly so. When they were playing, though, the story was different. The Cincinnati Reds traded Robinson, claiming he was too old at twenty-nine, because the club considered him to have a bad attitude. Pittsburgh Pirates management and the local media circulated similar complaints about Clemente. Both men were rapped as surly or moody, and both were plagued by rumors that their inevitable submission to slumps or late-season exhaustion stemmed from being weakened by the ravages of syphilis, thereby getting the black hypersexuality stereotype into the picture. What prompted these judgments? Both men simply sought to conduct themselves with a measure of dignity; they presumed a right to be treated with equal respect.

THE VIEW OF MANY BLACK ATHLETES

We don't know who the successful African American is anymore. We come out of a protest era, but the successful African American doesn't have much to protest—without much risk to his success. For the most part, he makes his living being the best at what he is. Their contribution is being the best. The time has passed when black athletes have that mantle of being a role model in black society. Increasingly, as do other successful blacks, they distance themselves from any acknowledged obligation to serve the interest of the black masses. These athletes have less and less in common with the black masses. Charles Barkley spoke for a lot of black athletes, perhaps an entire generation of black athletes, when he said "I'm not a role model."

Harry Edwards, ESPN Sports Zone transcript, http://espn.sportszone.com/editors/talk/transcripts/0911edwards.html

---

Booker T. Washington said blacks should be "patient suffering, slow to anger," and that is the downside of Jackie Robinson's legacy, though it's hardly his fault. The public imagery of Jackie Robinson's accomplishment and ordeal has been used as a justification for preaching quiescence in the name of moral superiority. Robinson's "quiet dignity" was frequently invoked, for example, against more aggressive black radicalism in the 1960s. (Even *The Nation*—in its continuing drive to become the respectably liberal, loyal edge of Clintonism—has published a ludicrous article exhorting blacks in South Carolina to draw on the race's legacy of demonstrated moral superiority and thus defuse the state's controversy over the public display of the Confederate battle flag by embracing the flag and revalorizing it as a symbol of a racially democratic New South.)

As a professional athlete and as a black person, Jackie Robinson fought to bring into existence a world in which he and others would be able to pursue their craft on an equal basis with everyone else, without the fetters of stereotypes or invidious, unfair expectations and double standards. A world, that is, in which a ballplayer would be simply a ballplayer. That quest—obviously just and proper in its own right—had much broader ramification in 1947. Why? Because a dynamic political movement spurred it along.

It's not only unreasonable and unfair to expect athletes to adopt any public role other than simply as athletes; it's also a waste of time.

PERIODICAL BIBLIOGRAPHY

The following articles have been selected to supplement the diverse views presented in this chapter. Addresses are provided for periodicals not indexed in the *Readers' Guide to Periodical Literature*, the *Alternative Press Index*, the *Social Sciences Index*, or the *Index to Legal Periodicals and Books*.

Frank DeFord	"Crossing the Bar," *Newsweek*, April 14, 1997.
Peter Dreier	"Remembering Jackie Robinson," *Tikkun*, March/April 1997.
Richard E. Lapchick	"Race and College Sport: A Long Way to Go," *Race & Class*, April–June 1995.
Richard E. Lapchick	"U.S. Sports Industry Falling Behind in Managing Diversity," *Street & Smith's SportsBusiness Journal*, April 27–May 3, 1998. Available from 120 W. Morehead St., Suite 310, Charlotte, NC 28202.
Andrea Lewis	"Oral Oaths in the Zone," *Third Force*, May/June 1996.
Andrea Lewis	"Sporting Racism," *Third Force*, January/February 1996.
Richard Lewis Jr.	"Racial Position Segregation: A Case Study of Southwest Conference Football, 1978 and 1989," *Journal of Black Studies*, March 1995.
Mark Maske	"Despite Progress, the Front Offices Are Still Largely White," *Washington Post National Weekly Edition*, April 7, 1997. Available from 1150 15th St. NW, Washington, DC 20071.
S.L. Price	"Is It in the Genes?" *Sports Illustrated*, December 8, 1997.
Steve Sailer	"Great Black Hopes," *National Review*, August 12, 1996.
Steve Sailer	"How Jackie Robinson Desegregated America," *National Review*, April 8, 1996.
Kenneth L. Shropshire	"Jackie Robinson's Legacy," *Emerge*, April 1997. Available from One BET Plaza, 1900 W. Place NE, Washington, DC 20018-1211.
Scott Stossel	"Who's Afraid of Michael Jordan?" *American Prospect*, May/June 1997.
Jack E. White	"Stepping Up to the Plate," *Time*, March 31, 1997.
Jason Gray Zengerle	"Hoop Schemes," *American Prospect*, May/June 1997.

CHAPTER 4

IS THERE SEXUAL
EQUALITY IN SPORTS?

Chapter Preface

The 1998 Winter Olympics in Nagano, Japan, featured the debut of women's ice hockey. Six teams competed, with the United States defeating Canada in the gold-medal game. Many writers praised the American women's triumph, but other people argued that women's hockey was not yet ready for the international arena.

Those who wish to see women's hockey remain a permanent part of the Olympics cited the purity of the game and the joyful attitudes of the athletes. These writers contrasted that behavior with the actions of the American men's team, which consisted of professional hockey players. That team performed far below expectations, failing to win a medal and trashing their rooms in the Olympic Village. The women's team was viewed as an example of the best that amateur sports have to offer. David Nyhan writes, "This inspiring athletic contest showcased sport at a higher level. . . . The rules for women's ice hockey make for a better, faster, more skillful and entertaining sport than do the rules for the men's version." Nyhan argued that the body checking and violent hits found in men's hockey mar that game.

However, the quality of women's hockey was not universally praised. Some people—including a few advocates—argued that women's ice hockey was not yet ready for the Olympics because of the poor caliber of play. The United States and Canada dominated the other four teams, scoring a combined fifty goals and giving up only eight. Scores such as 13-0 and 7-1 won games. However, some writers considered even the two best teams lacking. Douglas S. Looney, senior sports columnist for the *Christian Science Monitor*, writes, "The skills of the players, no matter which team, are works in progress. The sport isn't ready for prime time analysis by millions of television watchers." Looney cites the lack of physical play as a key drawback. Bernie Miklasz, a writer for the *St. Louis Post-Dispatch*, acknowledges the importance of women's ice hockey but notes that the play is mediocre and slow.

The addition of women's ice hockey to the Olympics is one example of the ongoing development of women's sports. In the following chapter, the authors debate whether this growth has led to sexual equality in sports.

"Thanks to pressure from the Clinton administration and the federal courts, schools are destroying men's athletics programs across the country."

TITLE IX IS UNFAIR TO MEN'S SPORTS

Elizabeth Arens

In the following viewpoint, Elizabeth Arens argues that enforcement of Title IX, which requires that men and women have equal opportunity to participate in intercollegiate sports, hinders men's athletic opportunities. Arens believes that more men than women are interested in taking part in college sports and that universities fail to take this into account when applying Title IX. Instead, Arens contends, universities enforce Title IX by cutting the number of men's teams in order to achieve a balance between the number of male and female athletes. As of 1998, Arens was a student at Princeton University in Princeton, New Jersey, and a member of the women's varsity squash team.

As you read, consider the following questions:

1. Previous to the publication of this viewpoint, how many men's athletic teams does Arens say have been eliminated because of Title IX?
2. In the author's opinion, why does gender "equity" make little sense at California State University at Bakersfield?
3. Why is proportionality difficult to achieve, according to the author?

Excerpted from Elizabeth Arens, "The Gender Refs," *Policy Review*, November/December 1997. Reprinted with permission of *Policy Review*.

When the men's varsity swimming and diving team at the University of California at Los Angeles performed in competition, they gave spectators more than a glimpse of athletic grace—they showed how disciplined greatness can emerge from eager but untrained youth. The team consistently finished among the nation's top 10. Over the years, it had secured 41 national titles in individual events and a National Collegiate Athletic Association (NCAA) championship. Members of the squad have won an astonishing 22 Olympic medals.

THE ELIMINATION OF MEN'S TEAMS

No more. The Olympic-size pools at UCLA are now closed to the male swimmers who set so many records there. In an apparent effort to achieve "gender equity" in collegiate athletics, university officials dropped the men's squad in 1993, making room for women's teams in soccer and water polo. The UCLA team was one of 16 NCAA men's swimming squads eliminated since 1993.

These programs join more than 200 men's athletics teams eliminated nationwide over the last several years. According to a survey by the NCAA, that amounts to a net loss of more than 17,000 opportunities for men in collegiate athletics.

Many of these teams are victims of misguided egalitarianism. Colleges and universities are misapplying a federal anti-discrimination statute to artificially equalize the number of men and women participating in collegiate athletics. Thanks to pressure from the Clinton administration and the federal courts, schools are destroying men's athletics programs across the country. They are capping the sizes of teams, terminating long-standing programs, and driving thousands of male students off the playing fields. And they are doing so without regard to the level of interest in sports demonstrated by female students or to the resources of the schools they attend.

TITLE IX HAS BEEN MISINTERPRETED

The source of this mischief is a distorted interpretation of Title IX, enacted by Congress as part of the 1972 Education Amendments. Intended to ensure that schools do not discriminate in providing athletic opportunities for their students, it states that "no person shall, on the basis of sex, be excluded from participation in, or denied the benefits of, or be subjected to discrimination under any educational program or activity receiving federal aid." On the face of it, it was a benign anti-discrimination statute.

In the hands of federal judges and officials at the U.S. Department of Education, however, the statute has become toxic for collegiate athletics. The department's Office of Civil Rights (OCR) has decided to judge compliance with the law not by whether colleges are practicing clear-cut discriminating but rather by [whether] they are failing to achieve "proportionality." In this case, proportionality means attaining a gender ratio among varsity athletes equal to that of the student body.

If that sounds like a quota, it is. Though the OCR's interpretation of the law was first issued in 1979, its application remained uncertain due to a Supreme Court decision in the mid-1980s. The mass elimination of men's teams began in the 1990s. "It's become really horrific since Clinton came into office," says Leo Kocher, a professor and wrestling coach at the University of Chicago. "The people in the OCR have really begun to interpret this as a quota law."

Federal courts have been only too eager to go along, cementing proportionality into law. Consider *Cohen v. Brown*, the most prominent Title IX case so far, which the Supreme Court declined to review in the spring of 1997. After Brown University eliminated two men's and two women's teams for budgetary reasons, female athletes sued in 1992 seeking to reinstate the women's teams.

Federal district judge Raymond Pettine ruled, and the appeals court affirmed, that as long as the proportion of women athletes was lower than the proportion of women students, Brown could not eliminate viable women's teams. Pettine further ordered Brown to "balance" its athletic program so that the proportion of female athletes equaled the proportion of female students. . . .

PROPORTIONALITY PROBLEMS

One way to achieve proportionality at a university is to place limits on the number of players on men's teams. Penn State, San Francisco State, the University of California at Berkeley, and the University of Colorado are just some of the schools that have placed such caps on men's participation. Coach T.J. Kerr's wrestling team at California State University at Bakersfield was capped at 25 members; he used to carry 37. . . .

The pursuit of gender "equity" in athletics makes little sense at a school like Bakersfield. Its student body is 64 percent female, but many of these women are students in their 40s or 50s who married young, had families, and later returned to college. Few exhibit any interest in participating in varsity athletics. But after the National Organization for Women (NOW) sued the California State University system in 1993, Bakersfield agreed to achieve proportionality in finance and participation by the 1998–99 school year.

At the time of the consent decree between NOW and the university system, 60 percent of varsity athletes at Bakersfield were male. "They were going to have to reverse that within five years," Kerr explains. To reach that goal, he says, the president recommended the elimination of men's wrestling and swimming teams in 1996. "They were trying to cut our two best sports—our flagship teams."

The team was saved temporarily, Kerr says, but "we're still fighting for our lives." He says the athletic department told him he would have to raise all the money for new scholarships himself. But after he set up an endowment for the team, he was told he couldn't use those funds. "They would have to increase expenditures for the women's teams," Kerr explains, "and they can't find the money to do that."

OTHER VICTIMS OF TITLE IX

Bakersfield's teams may have escaped the axe for now, but scores of men's teams have not. Indeed, eliminating men's teams—or demoting them and leaving them to wither away—is becoming the *modus operandi* of college officials eager to submit to federal regulators.

Consider the wrestling team at the State University of New York at Albany. In 1995 Albany cut wrestling, along with men's tennis, men's swimming, and women's swimming. Former coach Joe DeMeo has no doubt that compliance with Title IX was the motive for eliminating his team. "My athletic director said it was gender equity," he says. DeMeo's team had been another success story, producing five Olympians and suffering only one losing season over the past 18 years. "My athletes were tremendously disappointed," DeMeo says. "They worked really hard to keep the team alive."

Another successful program to die was UCLA's men's gymnastics team. It was demoted in 1993 to club status, where it receives minimal funding and cannot compete in NCAA championships. This program had produced, among others, Peter Vidmar, the winner of two gold medals and a silver medal at the 1984 Olympic games.

"The chancellor of the university told me personally that the team was cut so that [UCLA] could fall in line with Title IX," Vidmar says. "The gymnastics team was about second in the country when it was cut, and it had the highest academic average in the athletic department. But apparently these were not valid criteria for keeping the team." Vidmar is concerned about the future of his sport in this country. "I'm excited about all the opportunities for my daughters," he said, "but unless things change, my sons won't have a place to compete in gymnastics—there won't be any teams left."

THE IMPACT OF FOOTBALL

With the strict by-the-numbers approach of proportionality, says Bob Boettner, the executive director of the College Swimming Coaches Association, "it's become a simple equation—you either add women's sports or you eliminate men's sports. When administrators are faced with making ends meet, they'll do the latter." Sports that do not generate income from ticket sales or other sources—so-called nonrevenue sports—are usually the first to go: Between 1994 and 1996, NCAA schools eliminated 31 golf programs, 16 swimming programs, 22 tennis programs, 60 track programs, and 24 wrestling programs.

One of the few men's sports nearly immune to elimination is football. "Schools are not going to mess with their football teams," Kocher says. "Those are the big money makers."

Because most athletic departments spend a large portion of their budgets on their football programs, the sport has often been the target of feminists. Donna Lopiano of the Women's Sports Foundation has repeatedly lambasted universities for sacrificing women's sports and men's nonrevenue sports in order to protect their football and basketball programs. But football and basketball bring in extra cash for many athletic departments, providing funds for both men's and women's nonrevenue sports. NCAA data indicates that, in Division I-A, men's football and basketball generated income well in excess of their expenses. For all other sports, however, the reverse was true. In addition, many of the most thriving women's programs, such as those at Iowa and Ohio State, are found at schools with successful, profitable football teams.

WOMEN LACK INTEREST IN SPORTS

As men's opportunities disappear in the name of proportionality, mounting evidence suggests that women students may have less interest than men in participating in collegiate athletics. Disparities in the participation level of men and women exist even where the charge of historic discrimination against women would be very hard to support.

Vassar College, for example, is a former women's college that turned coeducational in 1969. Although its student population is

60 percent female, only 47 percent of its 299 varsity athletes are women—a proportionality gap of 13 percentage points. "We've had a lot of open spots that were not occupied on the rosters of women's teams," says Andy Jennings, the director of athletics.

In Auburn's swimming program, which maintains a men's team of 26 and a women's team of 21, the coach has had difficulty enlarging his women's team. "We're encouraged to increase women's participation," says David Marsh, "but it's difficult. There's substantially less interest on the women's side."

Fewer Opportunities for Male Athletes

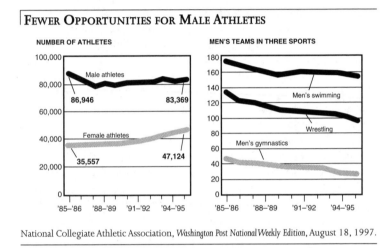

National Collegiate Athletic Association, *Washington Post National Weekly Edition*, August 18, 1997.

Mary Curtis, the associate athletic director and the coordinator of Title IX compliance at the University of Iowa, says that she has little difficulty attracting qualified female athletes. "There are more than enough athletes out there," she says. "But if you don't spend the recruiting money, you're not going to get the athletes."

But Marsh's experience suggests that money is not the only issue. Auburn offers 14 scholarships for female swimmers and only 10 for men, but still has fewer female swimmers. Marsh sees a clear unfairness in the allocation of scholarship funds. "An Olympic-level athlete on the men's side will receive significantly less than a female athlete of comparable ability. It's discouraging to the men, and it's not the greatest for the dynamics between my two teams."

Brown University's Evidence

In its defense in the *Cohen* case, Brown University submitted evidence suggesting that the pool of interested, qualified female athletes at the university and in the nation at large is significantly smaller than that for males. The evidence included a 1992 survey by the National Federation of State High Schools Association, which found that 3.5 million boys but only 2 million girls were members of high school varsity teams.

Brown also submitted for evidence College Board questionnaires filled out by high school students who had taken the SAT. Among SAT takers who had requested that their scores be sent to Brown, 50 percent of the male students, but only 30 percent of the women students, had expressed interest in participating in athletics. Brown's applicants at the time were more than 50 percent female, but of the applicants expressing interest in sports, less than 45 percent were women. And at Brown, as in the nation at large, the participants in intramural athletics, which are open to all students, are overwhelmingly male.

Such a survey of students' interest in athletics may not be an accurate measurement of the number who actually plan, and have the training and ability, to play on a varsity athletic team. Together with the data on high school and intramural participation, however, this evidence strongly suggests a real disparity in the levels of interest of each sex—one that would naturally lead to a gap in the number of male and female varsity athletes. But the proportionality requirement declares, in effect, that interest and ability do not matter. If not enough women can be encouraged to play sports, schools will have to cut down on male participation.

THE ORIGINAL INTENT OF TITLE IX

As it was originally written, Title IX did not create this problem. According to many who have been involved in women's athletics since the 1970s, Title IX has been a strong, constructive force propelling the growth of women's athletics. Charlotte West, a former president of the Association of Intercollegiate Athletics for Women, says that women's teams received "next to nothing from the universities" before Title IX. The funding and attention given to women's teams was "minuscule" compared with the men's, she says. "The treatment of women's teams by the universities was atrocious." West attributes much of the change of the past 25 years to Title IX, saying that "until the potential threat was there, it was difficult to get them to move."

In the decade after the passage of Title IX, women's collegiate sports boomed. The 1970s saw large gains in the number of women's teams, in the number of participants, and in funding. But recently, growth in the total number of female collegiate athletes nearly stopped, suggesting that the proportionality requirement is doing more to eliminate opportunities for male athletes than to benefit women. . . .

STRICT PROPORTIONALITY HAS PITFALLS

Fearing a lawsuit or an OCR "compliance review," college administrators have been all too ready to dispose of men's teams to meet the federal requirements. "I think many schools have misinterpreted Title IX, and I think they've taken the easy way out," says Jean Freeman at the University of Minnesota. She blames universities for "not using their creativity. They don't want to spend their time and energy, so they cut men's teams." Anne James, the women's swimming coach at the University of Arkansas, which dropped its men's team, agrees that "they're meeting the letter of the law, but not the spirit." Says Kocher, "The law is creating an enormous incentive for the elimination of male athletes."

At the heart of this scandal is the ascendancy of the strict proportionality requirement, slipped into the law by the OCR's 1979 policy interpretation. This requirement is found nowhere in the language of the original statute. In fact, Title IX explicitly states that nothing within the law should "be interpreted to require any educational institution to grant preferential or disparate treatment to one sex on account of an imbalance which may exist" in the numbers of each sex participating in a certain activity. Nor do the 1975 Title IX regulations, issued by the Department of Health, Education, and Welfare to flesh out the statute, mandate proportionality. On the contrary, these regulations require that schools examine "whether the selection of sports and levels of competition effectively accommodate the interests and abilities of members of both sexes."

Under the current interpretation, however, the respective "interests and abilities" of the two sexes are deemed irrelevant to the apportioning of varsity spots. In fact, Judge Pettine in Cohen v. Brown refused to admit much of Brown's statistical evidence related to the issue of interest and ability. "Even if it can be empirically demonstrated that, at a particular time, women have less interest in athletics than do men," wrote the judge, "such evidence, standing alone, cannot justify providing fewer athletic opportunities for women than for men." Such a ruling surely represents the triumph of ideology over fairness. . . .

BARRIERS TO PROPORTIONALITY

Why is proportionality so difficult to achieve? The lesser interest of female students is clearly a factor. Another is the large size of football teams, which places schools at an immediate disadvantage. At big-time football schools, teams often have as many as 120 members; no other sport, men's or women's, is comparable. In order to equalize the numbers, schools would need three or four more women's teams than men's (hence varsity bowling and synchronized swimming).

A barrier to achieving financial proportionality is the complicated system by which schools raise money for teams. Many teams receive money directly from booster clubs and alumni donors. Furthermore, certain teams require more funding simply because of the equipment that the sport requires. The Javits Amendment of 1974 directed that Title IX regulation must include "reasonable provisions considering the nature of particular sports," but this is an instruction that the OCR has largely ignored.

In his *Cohen v. Brown* decision, Pettine ruled that Brown could comply with Title IX in three ways. It could "elevate or create the requisite number of women's positions," it could "demote or eliminate the requisite number of men's positions," or it could "eliminate its athletic program altogether." Thankfully, schools have not chosen to take the third route. But, at a time when many universities are in financial distress, they have often been compelled to take the second. The federal interpretation has set up an artificial, clumsy, thoughtlessly egalitarian standard. The effort to achieve this standard is destroying men's athletic programs and eliminating men's opportunities across the nation.

| "Without [Title IX] enforcement, intercollegiate sports would still be a man's game."

TITLE IX IS NECESSARY FOR WOMEN AND IS NOT UNFAIR TO MEN'S SPORTS

Lynette Labinger

In the following viewpoint, Lynette Labinger, who represented female athletes in a class-action suit against Brown University, argues that Title IX—which guarantees women equal opportunities in education, including athletics—should not be weakened. She contends that, while participation by female athletes on the high school and college level has increased, women have not yet achieved equity. Labinger asserts that Title IX is still necessary and that equity can be reached without sacrificing men's sports.

As you read, consider the following questions:

1. According to Labinger, how many girls now participate in high school sports?
2. Who establishes athletic quotas, in Labinger's view?
3. According to Labinger, how did the federal court say Brown University could comply with Title IX?

Reprinted from Lynette Labinger, "Opportunities Aren't Equal for Women," *The New York Times*, September 17, 1995, p. A22, with permission from The TLPJ Foundation, a nonprofit membership organization supporting the work of Trial Lawyers for Public Justice, a national public interest law firm; website: www.tlpj.org.

1994's college women's basketball championships captured the imagination of sports fans nationwide, filling arenas and proving that women can be just as big a box-office draw as their male counterparts. But while women's college sports teams are attracting record-breaking crowds, Title IX—the statute responsible for the growth of women's intercollegiate athletics across the country—is under attack.

DO NOT WEAKEN TITLE IX

Weakening Title IX enforcement, however, would be a mistake. Without its enforcement, intercollegiate sports would still be a man's game.

Title IX of the Education Amendments of 1972 prohibits sex discrimination by all educational institutions receiving Federal funds. While it does not mandate that equal numbers of men and women participate in sports, it does require that men and women have equal opportunity to participate in sports and receive the benefits of competitive athletics.

In the early 1970's, before Title IX took hold, girls represented only 7.4 percent of high school athletes—under 300,000. Why? Because high schools discriminated against girls in their sports offerings. How can we be so sure that these low numbers were due to denial rather than a lack of interest? Because by 1976, the number of girls participating in high school sports had skyrocketed to 28.6 percent of all high school athletes—over 1.6 million. Today, over 2 million girls participate in high school sports programs and represent about 38 percent of high school athletes.

But despite these advances, women still haven't achieved equity. Women make up over one-half of college undergraduates yet constitute only one-third of all intercollegiate athletes.

THE SITUATION AT BROWN UNIVERSITY

My exposure to this issue dates back to 1991, when Brown University decided to cut two women's teams from its funded varsity program for strictly financial reasons. Brown terminated its women's gymnastics and volleyball teams—and also men's golf and water polo—as funded varsity sports in May 1991, but said they could continue to compete if the teams raised their funds. For the women's teams, that amount represented a loss of over $62,000; for the men, it was less than $16,000. As the evidence of trial later established, Brown expected the men's teams, but not the women's, to survive the cuts.

Members of the two women's teams turned to Trial Lawyers for Public Justice, a national public-interest law firm in Washington, for help. I agreed to serve as lead counsel in Rhode Island. Before filing a lawsuit, we met with Brown officials in an effort to convince them to reinstate the women's teams. We pointed out that Brown had not provided equal athletic opportunities for women before the cuts, that litigation was expensive, win or lose, and that the money would be better spent on athletes than on lawyers. After all, the whole issue started over money, not some weighty principle of law or academic philosophy.

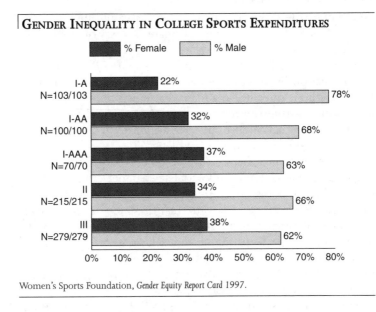

GENDER INEQUALITY IN COLLEGE SPORTS EXPENDITURES

Women's Sports Foundation, *Gender Equity Report Card 1997.*

But Brown refused, and we all became embroiled in a lawsuit in which Brown—long regarded as a bastion of progressive thought—has ironically taken the lead in championing sexist stereotypes and arguments that undermine women's progress in athletics. Sadly, Brown has already spent hundreds of thousands of dollars funding teams of lawyers to try to avoid spending tens of thousands on athletes.

UNFAIR ATTACKS ON TITLE IX

To make its case in court, Brown mounted a full-scale attack on Title IX. Brown joined other Title IX critics by raising the red herrings of "quotas" and "affirmative action" to attack it. The school said that fewer women than men participated in its sports programs because women have less interest and ability in sports. In reality, as the court found, Brown, like other universities, predetermines men's and women's athletic participation rates through its sports offerings, team sizes, coaches, recruiting and admission practices. In other words, if there is a "quota" involved here, it's established by the school, not Title IX.

Title IX opponents inaccurately claim that the law has been inflexibly interpreted to require colleges to provide athletic opportunities to men and women in proportion to undergraduate enrollment. But achieving "substantial proportionality" is only one way for a school to prove it is complying with Title IX. A school can also comply by demonstrating that it has continuously expanded its intercollegiate athletic program to meet women's developing interests and abilities, or that its current program "fully and effectively accommodates" women's interests and abilities.

After a lengthy trial in the fall of 1994, a Federal court ruled that Brown was in violation of Title IX because it failed all three tests. It specifically rejected Brown's claim that Title IX established quotas that would force the university to cut back on opportunities for men. The court noted that, unlike quotas, which require that established positions be filled with members of a disadvantaged group regardless of ability, Title IX allows schools to provide fewer opportunities for women when there is not sufficient interest and ability in creating more slots. The court held that Brown could comply with Title IX by providing fully funded varsity status to four women's teams that had demonstrated strong interest and ability even though women would still make up far less than 50 percent of the university's athletes.

THE WRONG APPROACH TO COMPLIANCE

Unfortunately, some universities would rather cut men's teams than expand opportunities for women. Brown has repeatedly threatened to do the same—an action that fuels political attacks on Title IX but does little to serve the interests of either male or female students. Instead, universities can comply with Title IX by reallocating resources within their athletic programs without cutting men's teams.

Why all the fuss? Playing sports helps both men and women develop self-confidence and self-esteem. And the availability of athletic scholarships gives many women the opportunity to obtain a college education—as it has historically done for men.

While women athletes on college campuses haven't yet achieved equity with their male counterparts, they've come a long way since Title IX's enactment. Title IX is working. It shouldn't be weakened because some universities would rather make excuses than give women their fair share.

| "The fastest women will never equal the fastest men in any standard-length race."

WOMEN ARE NOT AS ATHLETICALLY GIFTED AS MEN

Steve Sailer and Stephen Seiler

In the following viewpoint, Steve Sailer and Stephen Seiler claim that female athletes will never outperform their male counterparts. Using running events to compare the two sexes, the authors observe that the gap between men's and women's times in track races has increased during the 1990s. Sailer and Seiler assert that the growing gap is partly due to a decline in the number of African women competing in sports and stricter controls on steroid use by female runners from formerly Communist European nations. Sailer is a businessman and writer, and Seiler is a sports physiologist at Agder College in Kristiansand, Norway.

As you read, consider the following questions:

1. In the authors' views, why is track the best sport to use to compare men's and women's performances?
2. According to the authors, by what percentage did women Olympic medalists in the footraces become slower between 1988 and 1996?
3. What two events led to the crash of women's running, according to Sailer and Seiler?

Everybody knows that the gap in physical performance between male and female athletes is rapidly narrowing. In fact, in an opinion poll just before the 1996 Olympics, 66 per cent agreed that "the day is coming when top female athletes will beat top males at the highest competitive levels." The most highly publicized scientific study supporting this belief appeared in *Nature* in 1992: "Will Women Soon Outrun Men?" Physiologists Susan Ward and Brian Whipp pointed out that since the Twenties women's world records in running had been falling faster than men's. Assuming these trends continued, men's and women's records would equalize by 1998 for marathons, and during the early twenty-first century for all other distances. . . .

A LOOK AT THE NUMBERS

When everybody is so sure of something, it's time to update the numbers. So, we began an in-depth study.

Our conclusion: Although the 1998 outdoor running season has not yet started, we can already discard Ward and Whipp's forecast: women will not catch up to men in the marathon next year. The gender gap between the best marathon times remains the equivalent of the woman record holder's losing by more than 2.6 miles. In fact, we can now be certain that the fastest women will never equal the fastest men in any standard-length race. Contrary to all expectations, the overall gender gap has been widening throughout the Nineties. While men's times have continued to get faster, world-class women are running noticeably slower than in the Eighties. Why? It's a fascinating tale of sex discrimination, ethnic superiority, hormones, and the fall of the Berlin Wall that reconfirms the unpopular fact that biological differences between the sexes and the races will continue to play a large, perhaps even a growing, role in human affairs.

First, though, why is running the best sport for carefully measuring changes in the gender gap? For one thing, men and women currently compete under identical conditions in ten Olympic running events. In general, track is ideal for statistical study because it's such a simple sport: all that matters is the times. It's also probably the most universal sport. Track medalists in the 1996 Olympics included an Australian aborigine as well as runners from Burundi, Trinidad and Tobago, South Korea, Mozambique, Norway, and Namibia. Running is so fundamental to life and so cheap that most children on earth compete at it enough to reveal whether they possess any talent for it.

As Ward and Whipp noted, the gender gap did narrow sharply up through the Eighties. Let's focus on those ten directly comparable races. Back in 1970, women's world-record times averaged 21.3 per cent higher (worse) than men's. But in the Seventies women broke or equaled world records 79 times, compared to only 18 times for men, lowering the average gender gap in world records to 13.3 per cent. In the Eighties, women set 47 records compared to only 23 by men, and the gender gap shrank to just 10.2 per cent. Further narrowing seemed inevitable in the Nineties.

Yet male runners are now pulling away from female runners. Women's performances have collapsed, with only 5 record-setting efforts so far in the 1990s, compared to 30 by men. (The growth of the gender gap has even been accelerating. Men broke or tied records 7 times in 1997, the most in any year since 1968.) The average gender gap for world records has increased from 10.2 per cent to 11.0. And since four of the five women's "records" set in the Nineties occurred at extremely questionable Chinese meets (as we shall see later), it's probably more accurate to say that for relatively respectable records, men are ahead of women 30 to 1, and the average gender gap has grown from 10.2 per cent to 11.5 per cent.

Despite all the hype about 1996 being the "Women's Olympics," in the Atlanta Games' central events—the foot-races—female medalists performed worse relative to male medalists than in any Olympics since 1972. In the 1988 Games the gender gap for medalists was 10.9 per cent, but it grew to 12.2 per cent in 1996. Even stranger is the trend in absolute times. Track fans expect slow but steady progress; thus, nobody is surprised that male medalists became 0.5 per cent faster from the 1988 to the 1996 Olympics. Remarkably, though, women medalists became 0.6 per cent *slower* over the same period.

A LOOK AT ETHNICITY

Why is the gender gap growing? In the longer races—from 800m to the marathon, but especially in the 5,000m and 10,000m races—the main reason is discrimination, society forcing women to stay home and have six babies. Of course, we're not talking about the industrialized world, but about a few polygamous, high-birth-rate African nations. All 17 male distance record-settings in the Nineties belong to Africans— Kenyans (9), Ethiopians (5), Algerians (2), Moroccans (1). A culture can encourage women to pursue glory in athletics or to have a half-dozen kids, but not both. Thus, Kenya's high birth rate (not long ago it was more than five times West Germany's) has contributed to a swelling torrent of brilliant male runners, but has kept any Kenyan woman from winning Olympic gold.

These facts, though, raise a disturbing question: Why is women's distance running so debilitated by sexism in these African countries? Because, as Willie Sutton might say, that's where the talent is. You can't understand women's running without comparing it to men's running, and that has become incomprehensible unless you grasp how, as equality of opportunity has improved in men's track, ethnic inequality of result has skyrocketed. The African tidal wave culminated on August 13, 1997, when Wilson Kipketer, a Kenyan running for Denmark, broke the great Sebastian Coe's 800m mark, erasing the last major record held by any man not of African descent. African superiority is now so manifest that even Burundi, a small East African hell-hole, drubbed the U.S. in the men's distance races at our own Atlanta Games.

COMPARING MEN'S AND WOMEN'S TRACK RECORDS

	Distance	Record	Nation	Date
Men	100 meters	9.84 seconds	Canada	7-27-96
Women	100 meters	10.49 seconds	U.S.	7-16-88
Men	200 meters	19.32 seconds	U.S.	8-01-96
Women	200 meters	21.34 seconds	U.S.	9-29-88
Men	400 meters	43.29 seconds	U.S.	8-17-88
Women	400 meters	47.60 seconds	East Germany	10-06-85
Men	800 meters	1:41.11 minutes	Denmark	8-24-97
Women	800 meters	1:53.28 minutes	Czechoslovakia	7-26-83
Men	1 mile	3:44.39 minutes	Algeria	9-05-93
Women	1 mile	4:12.56 minutes	Russia	8-14-96
Men	Marathon	2:06:50 hours	Ethiopia	4-17-88
Women	Marathon	2:21:06 hours	Norway	4-21-85

International Amateur Athletics Federation (IAAF), recognized records as of July 15, 1998, http://www.usatf.org/athletes/world.shtml.

Yet, there are striking systematic differences even between African ethnic groups. This can best be seen by graphing each population's bell curve for running. The Olympic events from 100 meters to the marathon run along the horizontal axis, and the percentage of the 100 best times in history go along the vertical axis. For example, the distances Kenyan men are best suited for are indicated by a bell curve centered on the 3,000m steeple-chase, where Kenyans own the 53 fastest times ever. These East

Africans are outclassed in the 100m and 200m, but become competitive in the 400m, then are outstanding from 800m through 10,000m, before tailing off slightly in the marathon (42,000m).

In contrast, for the black men of West Africa and the West African Diaspora (living, e.g., in the U.S., Nigeria, Cuba, Brazil, Canada, Britain, and France), only the right half of their bell curve is visible. They absolutely monopolize the 100m. Men of West African descent have broken the 10-second barrier 134 times; nobody else has *ever* done it. They remain almost as overwhelming in the 200m and 400m, then drop off to being merely quite competitive in the 800m. They are last sighted in the 1500m, and then are absolutely not a factor in the long-distance events.

While there are the usual nature v. nurture arguments over why African runners win so much, there is little possibility that culture alone can account for how much West African and East African runners differ in power v. endurance. Track is ultracompetitive: coaches test all their runners at different distances until they find where they are best. Even in the unlikely event that Kenya's coaches were too self-defeating to exploit their 100m talent, and Jamaica's leadership was ignoring their 10,000m prodigies, American and European coaches and agents would swoop in and poach them. No, what's far more plausible is that both West and East Africans are performing relatively close to their highly distinct biological limits.

FEARS OF RACIAL SUPREMACY

None of this conforms to American obsessions about race. First, we dread empirical studies of human biodiversity, worrying that they will uncover the intolerable reality of racial supremacy. Is this fear realistic? Consider merely running: Are West Africans generally better runners than whites? In sprints, absolutely. In distance races, absolutely not. Overall racial supremacy is nonsense; specific ethnic superiorities are a manifold reality.

Second, our crude racial categories blur over many fascinating genetic differences between, for example, groups as similar in color as West and East Africans. And even within the highlands of East Africa there are different track bell curves: Ethiopians, while almost as strong as Kenyans at 5,000m and longer, are not a factor below 3,000m. And the African dominance is not just a black thing. Moroccans and Algerians tend to be more white than black, yet they possess a bell curve similar to, if slightly less impressive than, Kenyans'. Further research will uncover many more fascinating patterns: for example, Europeans appear to be consistently mediocre, achieving world-class performances primarily at distances like 800m and the marathon that fall outside of the prime ranges for West Africans and Kenyans.

These ethnic patterns among male runners are crucial to understanding the causes of the growth in the gender gap, because it appears that women runners possess the same natural strengths and weaknesses as their menfolk. For example, the bell curves for men and women runners of West African descent are equally sprint-focused. If a nation's women perform very differently from its men, something is peculiar. With high-birth-rate African countries like Kenya and Morocco, it's clear that the social systems restrain marriageable women from competing. This offers hope that the distance gender gap will someday stop widening. Indeed, since the Kenyan birth rate began dropping a few years back, we have begun to see a few outstanding Kenyan women.

WOMEN'S RUNNING HAS DECLINED

The gender gap is widening not just because men (especially African distance runners) are running faster today, but also because women (especially East European sprinters) are now running slower.

From 1970 to 1989, white women from Communist countries accounted for 71 of the 84 records set at 100m–1500m. In contrast, Eastern European men accounted for exactly zero of the 23 male records. Those memorable East German Fräuleins set records 49 times in just the sprints and relays (100m–400m). This was especially bizarre because men of West African descent were utterly dominating white men in sprinting. Another oddity of that era is that Communist women set only 7 (and East Germans none) of the 48 female records in the 5k, 10k, and marathon.

The crash of women's running was brought about by two seemingly irrelevant events in the late Eighties: Ben Johnson got caught, and the Berlin Wall fell. At the 1988 Olympics, in the most anticipated 100m race of all time, Johnson, the surly Jamaican-Canadian sprinter who could benchpress 396 pounds, demolished Carl Lewis with a jaw-dropping world record of 9.79 seconds. Two days later Johnson was stripped of his medal and record because his urine contained steroids. Embarrassed that it had let a man called "Benoid" by other runners (his massively muscled body was so flooded with artificial male hormones that his eyeballs had turned yellow) become the biggest star in the sport, track officialdom finally got fairly serious about testing for steroids in 1989.

WOMEN AND STEROIDS

Then the Berlin Wall fell, and we learned exactly how East German coaches enabled white women to outsprint black women: by chemically masculinizing them. The East German regime understood that sports success is based on manliness, which (in its lowest-common-denominator definition of muscles and aggression) isn't a social but a biochemical construct, one that their technicians could churn out by the liter. Obviously, the Communists weren't the only dopers, but they were the best organized. Newsweek reported, "Under East Germany's notorious State Plan 14.25, more than 1,000 scientists, trainers, and physicians spent much of the 1980s developing better ways to drug the nation's athletes." East German coaches are now finally going on trial for forcing enormous doses of steroids on uninformed teenagers. The Soviet Union, although less brilliant in the laboratory, also engaged in cheating on an impressively industrial scale.

Even today, this pattern of women's records coming mostly from Communist countries continues: four of the 1990s' five female marks were set by teenagers at the Chinese National Games, where tough drug testing is politically impossible. (The 1997 Games in Shanghai were such a bacchanal of doping that all 24 women's weightlifting records were broken, but weightlifting's governing officials had the guts to refuse to ratify them.) In contrast to the astounding accomplishments by China's fuel-injected women, Chinese men's performances remain mediocre.

Both the East German and the Chinese Communists were almost completely stumped at concocting male champions because the benefits of a given amount of steroids are much greater for women than for men. Since men have on average 10 times more natural testosterone than women, they need dangerously large Ben Johnson-sized doses to make huge improvements, while women can bulk up significantly on smaller, less easily detected amounts. The primitive testing at the 1988 Olympics did catch Benoid.

Rumors also circulated around the female star of those Games, America's Florence Griffith-Joyner. From 1984 to 1987 the lissome Flo-Jo kept finishing second in big races to suspiciously brawny women. After asking Ben Johnson for training advice, she made a magnificent joke out of women's track in 1988, setting records in the 100m and 200m that few had expected to see before the middle of the twenty-first century. Yet, she passed every urinalysis she ever faced and retired just before random drug testing began in 1989.

Why didn't the East German labs synthesize successful women distance runners? Although artificial male hormones are somewhat useful to distance runners (in part because they increase the will to win), sprinters get the biggest bang for their steroid buck. The shorter the race, the more it demands anaerobic power (which steroids boost), while the longer the race, the more it tests aerobic and heat-dispersal capacities.

Doping has not disappeared from track, but runners have responded to better testing by using fewer steroids, and by trying less potent but harder-to-detect drugs like Human Growth Hormone. These new drugs affect the sexes much more equally than Old King Steroid. The decline in steroid use has allowed the natural order to reassert itself: before steroids overwhelmed women's track in the Seventies, black women like Wilma Rudolph and Wyomia Tyus dominated sprinting. Today, led by young Marion Jones, who is potentially the Carl Lewis of women's track, black women rule once more. However, white women are still much more heavily represented among the top sprinters than are white men. This could mean that the ethnic gap in natural talent between West Africans and Europeans is smaller among women than men. Or, more likely, doping continues to enhance women's times more than men's. If testing can continue to improve faster than doping, the gender gap would tend to grow even wider.

"In sports, as in the rest of life,
women do compete with men on a
daily basis, and often win."

WOMEN CAN BE AS ATHLETICALLY GIFTED AS MEN

Mariah Burton Nelson

In the following viewpoint, Mariah Burton Nelson argues that
the performances of women are equal to, and in some cases better than, those of men in most sports. She contends that men
have advantages in sports that emphasize upper-body strength
but claims that sports such as ultramarathon running and swimming, which require stamina, are more likely to have female
participants who triumph in head-to-head competition. Nelson
asserts that women's performances will improve as they are
given more opportunities to compete. Nelson is a former professional basketball player and the author of *The Stronger Women Get,
the More Men Love Football: Sexism and the American Culture of Sports*, the
book from which this viewpoint is taken.

As you read, consider the following questions:

1. According to the author, how are men the weaker sex?
2. Why does fat help women in long-distance races, according
   to Nelson?
3. For every woman who receives a college scholarship, how
   many men do, according to the author?

Two scientists made this forecast: The fastest woman may eventually outrun the fastest man. Their prediction appeared only as a letter to the editor in *Nature* magazine, yet it generated a stampede of interest from the media. *Time*, the *Chicago Tribune*, *USA Today*, the *New York Times*, the *Washington Post*, and *Sports Illustrated* printed stories. All quoted experts who ridiculed the conjecture as "ludicrous," "sheer ignorance," "a good laugh," "absurd," "asinine," "completely fallacious," and/or "laughable."

A RIDICULED REPORT

In one Associated Press report, the word ridiculous was used five times. *Science News* ran the headline "Women on the verge of an athletic showdown." *Runner's World* entitled its article "Battle of the Sexes." Unlike questionable projections that are dismissed without fanfare, this one seems to have struck a nerve.

The researchers, Brian Whipp and Susan Ward of the University of California, Los Angeles, calculated runners' average speeds during record-breaking races over the past seventy years, then compared the rates of increase. Noting that women's average speeds are increasing at a faster rate than are men's, they projected that in the future, the best women may catch up to and even surpass the best men at various distances. For example: By 1998, the best woman and man would, if they continue to improve at current rates, complete the 26.2-mile marathon in two hours, two minutes. In subsequent years, the woman would sprint ahead.

Indisputably, neither women nor men will continue to improve at their current rates forever. Otherwise, humans would one day run the marathon in a matter of minutes. But the very idea that women might someday beat men elicited passionate responses. *Runner's World* writers Amby Burfoot and Marty Post, as if verbally to stop women in their tracks, pointed out that in the past five years, women have made few improvements in world-record times. This is a sure sign, they said, that women "have already stopped" improving.

SOME MEN ARE ANGRY

When I appear on radio and television shows to discuss women's sports or my first book, *Are We Winning Yet? How Women Are Changing Sports and Sports Are Changing Women*, I encounter a similar fury. Female callers are not the problem; they brag about their triceps or gripe about male egos or ask for advice about discrimination. Some male callers tell stories about female martial artists or mountain climbers who taught them, in a way they could understand, about female strength. But at least half of the male callers act as if my views were heretical. Angry and antagonistic, they belittle me, my ideas, my book, and female athletes in general.

What seems to make them angriest is my observation that men are not better athletes than women are. In no sport are all men better than all women, I point out, and in many sports, women routinely defeat men. Although single-sex competitions are often appropriate, and men do have physical advantages in some sports, women should see themselves as men's peers, I suggest, rather than exclusively competing against women.

These men don't want to hear any of that. In voices I can only describe as high-pitched and hysterical, they say, "Yeah, but you're never going to see a woman play pro football!"

FOOTBALL IS OVEREMPHASIZED

It is a taunt and, I think, a genuine fear. I'm not talking about football. I've never met a woman who aspires to play pro football. I'm talking about auto racing, horse racing, dog sled racing, equestrian events, rifle shooting, and marathon swimming, where women and men compete together at the elite levels. I'm talking about tennis, golf, racquetball, bowling, skiing, and other recreational sports, where a wife and husband or a female and male pair of friends are likely to find themselves evenly matched. In sports, as in the rest of life, women do compete with men on a daily basis, and often win.

So it intrigues me that in response to my discussion of women's athletic excellence, men change the subject to football. They try to assert football as the sine qua non of athleticism. Because "women could never play football," they imply, men are physically, naturally, biologically superior.

Most men can't play pro football themselves—but they can take vicarious comfort in the display of male physical competence and aggression. . . .

Psychiatrist Arnold R. Beisser explains the phenomenon this way: "It is small wonder that the American male has a strong affinity for sports. He has learned that this is one area where there is no doubt about sexual differences and where his biology is not obsolete. Athletics help assure his difference from women in a world where his functions have come to resemble theirs."

MEN HAVE WEAKNESSES

Sports are about distinction. Who is better? One inch, one point, or one-hundredth of a second can differentiate winner from loser. One pound, one meal, one more set of two-hundred-meter sprints in practice can determine, or seem to determine, whether a person finishes first or last. Athletes may train for the sheer joy of moving their bodies through space, but eventually they grow curious to see how fast they can move, or how well they can perform, compared to others. They want to compare, to contrast, to differentiate. To know where they stand. To win.

THE TRAITS OF FEMALE ENDURANCE

What truly makes the female endurance competitor distinctive among the athletically elite is the way she trains her mind to override the pain that is almost always an accessory to ultra-marathoning. It's not mind over matter, nor is it as simple as visualizing oneself crossing the finish line. Rather, the ability to vanquish physical distress—in other words, to simply get over it—seems to be a particularly female quality, whether innate or a psychosocial construct.

Anngel Delaney, *On the Issues*, Fall 1998.

It is in this comparative, competitive arena that we are repeatedly told that women and men are different. And men are better. Women may no longer be weak, granted, but they are still weaker. Weaker than men. Still the weaker sex.

Still, as Simone de Beauvoir said, the second sex.

Actually, in many ways, men are the weaker sex. Men die on average seven years earlier than women. Women have a better sense of smell, taste, hearing, and sight (colorblindness affects one woman for every sixteen men). Women are more susceptible to migraines, arthritis, and depression, but men commit suicide more and have higher rates of heart attack and stroke. "Women are sick, but men are dead," Edward Dolnick wrote in his *In Health* magazine article on the subject.

Yet men keep pointing to one physical advantage—upper-body strength—to maintain their illusion of supremacy. Sports that depend on such strength—that, indeed, were designed to showcase that strength—bolster the myth.

MALE DISADVANTAGES IN SPORTS

Those who claim male sports superiority are not thinking of male gymnasts, who lack the flexibility to use some of the apparatus women use. Or male swimmers, who can't keep up with women over long distances. Or male equestrians, who gallop side by side with—or in the dust of—their female peers.

They are not considering how much women and men have

in common: the human experience of sport. These same people would never think of comparing Sugar Ray Leonard to Muhammad Ali. One weighed sixty pounds more than the other. Clearly, they deserved to box in different classes. Yet the top female tennis player is often compared to the top male tennis player ("Yeah but, she could never beat him"), who usually outweighs her by sixty pounds.

Those who claim male superiority are not remembering jockstraps. Because men's genitals dangle precariously outside the pelvis, they are vulnerable to speeding baseballs and to angry fists or feet. In addition, "bikes with dropped handlebars bring the rider's legs close to the stomach, and the testicles can get squashed or twisted against the saddle," notes sportswriter Adrianne Blue in *Faster, Higher, Further*. "This can lead to gangrene and amputation." Such cases have been noted in medical journals.

Blue also suggests that men's bigger bodies make more "dangerous missiles" that are more likely than women's bodies to cause injury when they collide. For this reason a case could be made, she says, for banning men from contact sports.

WOMEN CAN DEFEAT MEN

If women and men were to compete together in noncontact sports, a man would currently win at the elite levels of most existing events: running (as long as the race is under 100 miles); swimming (under about 22 miles); throwing shot, discus, or javelin. On average, men can carry and use more oxygen. They tend to be heavier—an advantage in football—and taller: handy in basketball and volleyball. Men have more lean muscle mass, convenient in sports requiring explosive power—which happens to include most of the sports men have invented.

Less muscle-bound, women generally have better flexibility, useful in gymnastics, diving, and skating. Our lower center of gravity can help in hockey, golf, tennis, baseball, and even basketball. We sweat better (less dripping, therefore better evaporation), which is critical since, like car engines, human bodies need to remain cool and well lubricated to function efficiently.

Physiologist Diane Wakat, associate professor of health education at the University of Virginia, tested athletes under various conditions of heat, humidity, exercise, and nutritional intake, and concluded that women are better able to adjust to the environmental changes. "In every case, females were better able to handle the stress," says Wakat.

The longer the race, the better women do. Women's superior insulation (fat) is, believe it or not, prized by some because it offers buoyancy, heat retention, and efficient use of fuel over long distances, whether by land or by sea.

WOMEN CAN OUTRUN AND OUTSWIM MEN

Ann Trason, a California microbiology teacher, became in 1989 the first woman to win a coed national championship—the twenty-four-hour run—by completing 143 miles. The best male finisher completed four fewer miles. Of Ward and Whipp's prediction that women will one day hold the overall world record in the relatively short (26.2-mile) marathon, Trason says: "I'd be there and be really happy to see it, but it seems unlikely. I do think women will get closer."

Helen Klein's world-record distance in a twenty-four-hour race—109.5 miles—exceeds the best distance for an American man in her age group (65–69). She says of the possibility that a woman will one day set the overall marathon record, "I would not say no. There is hope. If I were younger, I might try it myself."

In marathon and long-distance cold-water swims, "women usually outswim the men," says Bob Duenkel, curator of the International Swimming Hall of Fame. Penny Dean still holds the English Channel record she set in 1978. Diana Nyad is the only athlete to complete the swim from Bimini to Florida. Lynne Cox holds the records for swimming the Bering Strait and the Strait of Magellan. The first person to swim all five Great Lakes, and the first ever to cross Lake Superior (in 1988), was Vicki Keith.

Susan Butcher has been the overall winner of the 1,100-mile Iditarod dog sled race four times. A woman named Seana Hogan recently cycled the four hundred miles from San Francisco to Los Angeles in nineteen hours, forty-nine minutes, breaking the previous men's record by almost an hour.

EXPLAINING THE GENDER DIFFERENCES

But women's successes are rarely attributable to gender. In ultra-distance running, swimming, and cycling, as well as in equestrian events, horse racing, auto racing, and dog sled racing, success is determined primarily by physical and mental preparation, competitive spirit, self-discipline, or other nongender-related factors. Because upper-body strength is not paramount in these sports, women and men become free to compete together as individuals, even at the highest levels of competition.

Men's strength advantage is actually marginal, meaning that there is more variation among individual men than between the average man and the average woman. It only becomes relevant when comparing trained, competitive athletes. On any recreational doubles tennis team, the female player might be stronger.

Age is also important. Men's strength advantage occurs primarily during the reproductive years. Before puberty, girls, who tend to mature faster, have a height and strength advantage which, if not nullified by institutional and cultural discrimination, would actually render the best of them superior to the best boys. In old age, there is little physical difference between female and male strength. . . .

WOMEN'S AMBITIONS

Does it make any sense to ask whether women—even marathoners—will catch up to men? Most women don't think so.

"Let's just run as fast as we can and not compare ourselves to men," proposes Henley Gibble, executive director of the Road Runners Club of America. "It seems like a silly thing to do anyway. In the open distances, we're already winning."

"It's only relevant for me in terms of, Have women been given the same opportunities to explore what their own potential is?" says sports psychologist and University of Virginia professor Linda Bunker. "The bottom line—Will women ever be as good as men?—is not necessarily of interest."

Men are arrogant to think we want to catch up to them, says Susan Birrell, a trailblazing sports sociologist from the University of Iowa. "As if we don't have any ambition at all. As if all we want to do is catch up to men. Remember that quote: 'Women who want to be equal to men lack ambition.'"

ANN TRASON'S VIEWS

In addition to being the overall winner of the twenty-four-hour race, Ann Trason has five times won the women's division and in 1992 and 1993 finished third overall in the Western States 100-Mile Endurance Run. I ask her: "The whole concept of women catching up to men is off the mark for you, because you're already beating men, right?"

"I guess you could look at it that way," she replies. "That's sort of nice."

"Is it nice?" I ask. "Does it matter?"

"Yeah, it is important to me," she says. "It shows what women can do. It's not like I go out there intentionally to outrun men, but I'm proud of that achievement."

Male competitors have told Trason they'd "rather die" than "let" her pass them. But for Trason, competitions are not "athletic showdowns" or "battles of the sexes." In fact, the races nearly transcend gender, which appeals to her. "The nice thing about ultras [one-hundred-mile or twenty-four-hour races] is, you're just competing against whoever's out there. The sex barrier comes down. It's not gone altogether, but it's a lot less than if you were doing a 10K."

WOMEN'S OPPORTUNITIES HAVE BEEN LIMITED

Because "being masculine" has included access to diverse sporting opportunities and "being feminine" has not, it's shortsighted to postulate that current gaps between male and female athletic potential will not close, at least partially, in the future— or that, as Post and Burfoot asserted, women "have already stopped improving." Men prevented women from running marathons until 1967. The Olympics did not offer a women's marathon until 1984, and still doesn't offer a women's swimming event longer than eight hundred meters (the men swim fifteen hundred meters). For every college woman who gets a chance to play college sports, 2.24 men do. For every woman who receives a college scholarship, 2.26 men do. The more women run, the greater the likelihood that some of them will run fast. Increased numbers of female runners—along with female-focused training, coaching, scholarships, equipment, and even clothing—account for the historical improvements in women's times, and greater numbers in the future are likely to improve times further.

If marathon swimming were our national sport, as it is in Egypt—if there were a nationally televised Super Bowl of marathon swimming, and spectators packed college swim meets like sardines—we might think differently about women's and men's athletic capabilities. If men competed against women on the balance beam, or in synchronized swimming, or in rhythmic gymnastics, we might rephrase the question about who might catch up to whom.

Maybe, in a world where gender differences were no more relevant than hand sizes, we could innocently wonder if the best women will catch up to the best men in running while also pondering the possibility that the best men will catch up to the best women in gymnastic floor exercise. Neither would have emotional import.

But in this society, the question of women catching up to men has enormous emotional significance. Scientific inquiry is always influenced by the value system of the scientists: What questions are asked? Since most women runners express no desire to "catch up" to men, and indeed seem to want to avoid the comparison, more appropriate questions might be, Do women feel behind? If so, why? In what ways?

We might ask how many women will ultimately have opportunities to play sports. By what date will the percent of college women athletes—currently about one-third—reflect the percent of college women students—one-half? When will women "catch up" in terms of social support?

We might also ask why was the outcry about the letter to the editor of *Nature* far greater than the outcry about the National Collegiate Athletic Association's comprehensive study that described vast gender inequities in college sports.

PERIODICAL BIBLIOGRAPHY

The following articles have been selected to supplement the diverse views presented in this chapter. Addresses are provided for periodicals not indexed in the *Readers' Guide to Periodical Literature*, the *Alternative Press Index*, the *Social Sciences Index*, or the *Index to Legal Periodicals and Books*.

James Deacon with Scott Steele	"Leagues of Their Own: Women Are Finally Breaking the Old Boy Stranglehold on Sport," *Maclean's*, April 7, 1997.
E.J. Dionne Jr.	"Title IX and Changing Social Attitudes," *Liberal Opinion Week*, June 2, 1997. Available from PO Box 880, Vinton, IA 52349-0880.
Paul Farhi	"Courting the Women," *Washington Post National Weekly Edition*, November 17, 1997. Available from 1150 15th St. NW, Washington, DC 20071.
Don Feder	"Gender Jacobins Decapitate College Sports," *Conservative Chronicle*, May 7, 1997. Available from PO Box 29, Hampton, IA 50441.
Jane Gottesman	"Coverage of Women in Sports: Q & A with Championship Basketball Coach Tara VanDerveer," *Extra!* November/December 1994.
John Leo	"Gender Police: 'Pull Over!'" *U.S. News & World Report*, March 23, 1998.
Brenda Lichtman	"Sexual Discrimination and School Sports: The Title IX Compliance Challenge," *USA Today*, March 1998.
David Nakamura	"Male Athletes Find That Gender Equity Has Its Price," *Washington Post National Weekly Edition*, August 18, 1997.
Martina Navratilova	"Game, Set, Set, Set, Match," *New York Times*, August 26, 1996.
Martina Navratilova	"Men and Women in Sports: The Playing Field Is Far from Level," *USA Today*, November 1996.
David Nyhan	"Women Show U.S. How Real Hockey Should Be Played," *Liberal Opinion Week*, March 9, 1998.
Walter Olson	"Title IX from Outer Space: How Federal Law Is Killing Men's College Sports," *Reason*, February 1998.

Kate Rounds	"Tying the Score," *Ms.*, July/August 1997.
Joannie M. Schrof	"A Sporting Chance?" *U.S. News & World Report*, April 11, 1994.
David Tell	"Playing Unfair," *Weekly Standard*, July 7, 1997.
Steve Wulf	"A Level Playing Field for Women," *Time*, May 5, 1997.

CHAPTER 5

IS DRUG USE A PROBLEM IN SPORTS?

CHAPTER PREFACE

One of the biggest sports stories of 1998 was the pursuit of Roger Maris's single-season home run record in baseball. To the surprise of few baseball fans, one athlete leading the hunt was Mark McGwire of the St. Louis Cardinals. McGwire has long been one of baseball's most prolific sluggers, beginning with a rookie season in which he hit forty-nine home runs. On September 8, 1998, McGwire hit his sixty-second home run of the season, breaking Maris's mark; he finished the year with seventy home runs.

However, McGwire's admission in August 1998 that he had been using androstenedione, a testosterone-boosting compound, for over a year sparked a debate over the role of drugs in sports and whether McGwire's efforts or image was cheapened by the use of the drug. Major League Baseball permits the use of androstenedione, but the National Football League and other athletic organizations have banned it. [In December 1998, Major League Baseball commissioned a study on the drug's effects. They were to announce a decision on the future legality of androstenedione in spring 1999.]

Some observers argue that while McGwire is not breaking any rules, his use of androstenedione is troubling because he is considered to be a role model. In addition, these critics contend, McGwire risks having his record tainted. In an article in *Time* written before McGwire broke the record, Christine Gorman observed, "While it's perfectly legal . . . for McGwire to take the supplements, it sends an absolutely wrong health message to kids everywhere. If he does beat Roger Maris's home-run record, there will always be—for me, anyway—a mental asterisk next to his name."

Other writers acknowledge that baseball needs to reconsider its rules concerning androstenedione, but they maintain that McGwire's efforts should not be denigrated. These critics argue that other players take the compound, and they add that McGwire has always been a talented home run hitter. In a *New York Times* sports column, Ira Berkow writes, "McGwire has an obvious, and remarkable, natural athletic talent. . . . And he has continued to work on it, and his body, with, apparently, an uncommon devotion."

The controversy over Mark McGwire is just one aspect of the issue of drug use in sports. In the following chapter, authors debate whether drug use by athletes is a serious problem.

| "The use of banned performance-
enhancing drugs by elite athletes is
clearly widespread."

BANNING DRUGS FROM SPORTS IS IMPORTANT

Christopher Clarey

In the following viewpoint, Christopher Clarey contends that drug use by elite athletes is prevalent. He asserts that athletes use performance-enhancing substances because they believe their competitors are also likely to be using drugs. Besides altering the competitions, Clarey suggests that the pervasiveness of athletic drug use also limits the spectators' sense of wonder because remarkable performances become immediately suspect. Clarey is a contributing editor for *Tennis* magazine and a writer for the *International Herald Tribune*, an international newspaper based in Paris.

As you read, consider the following questions:

1. According to a survey of 198 athletes, as cited by the author, how many would take a banned performance-enhancing drug if they could be guaranteed victory without being caught?
2. In Clarey's view, why are sports organizations unable to end the drug problem?
3. Why do sports inspire, according to the author?

Reprinted from Christopher Clarey, "Doping Numbs the Sense of Wonder: Spectators Cannot Admire Champions Who Win by Fraudulent Means," *International Herald Tribune*, August 8, 1998, by permission of The New York Times Syndicate.

Perhaps Michelle Smith-De Bruin is guilty of tampering with her own urine samples. Perhaps not. Whatever the result of her appeal in the courts, whatever the merits of her four-year ban from swimming, international sport is unquestionably guilty.

The use of banned performance-enhancing drugs by elite athletes is clearly widespread, maybe even close to universal in some sports. For too many years and too many Olympiads, the rewards have been too great and the risk of getting caught too slight to dissuade would-be medalists.

PROMINENT DRUG SCANDALS

We are at another crossroads in August 1998. Doping scandals turned 1998's Tour de France into a very different sort of pursuit, and now De Bruin has been suspended from her sport by Federation Internationale De Natation Amateur (FINA), swimming's governing body.

A triple gold medalist at the 1996 Summer Olympics, De Bruin is arguably the most prominent sports figure to be banned since the Canadian sprinter Ben Johnson tested positive for steroids at the 1988 Games. There have been others, including Lyubov Yegorova, the Russian cross-country skier, who has won a record six Winter Olympic golds and was banned for three years after she tested positive for Bromantan at 1997's world Nordic championships.

Fraud—and that is what drug cheats are engaging in—should not go unpunished, and public humiliation and loss of earning power would normally appear to be effective deterrents. The problem is that the current system punishes so few of the guilty and makes those whom it does punish look like lonely villains instead of flawed protagonists with plenty of company on the moral low ground.

DRUGS ARE NOT DISDAINED BY ATHLETES

Johnson's ban set off a flurry of bureaucratic activity and official hand-wringing, but a decade later it is clear that Johnson's fall from grace was no turning point, merely part of a continuum and, in some insidious way, an inspiration.

How else to explain that in 1995, when 198 elite—mostly American—athletes were polled on whether they would take a banned performance-enhancing substance if they could be guaranteed that they would win and not be caught, 195 said they would do it. The athletes, who kept their anonymity, were also asked what they would do if a banned substance guaranteed they would win every competition they entered for the next five years and then later cause them to die from the side effects. About half said that they would take the substance.

That is the climate we are dealing with here. These young and gifted people have a case of tunnel vision and an oddly persuasive and self-soothing moral escape hatch: If so many others are taking these drugs, why shouldn't I? If those who oversee and organize sports cannot make the playing field level, why shouldn't I take matters into my own hands?

The Non-thinker.

The International Olympic Committee is again bustling about. A special meeting of the Executive Board was called for August 1998, and the International Olympic Committee president, Juan Antonio Samaranch, is tentatively planning a conference on drugs for January in Switzerland. (Conferences are a Samaranch specialty). [At the meeting, an anti-drug agency was proposed and the summit was set for February 1999.] But the truth is that sports organizations have demonstrated neither the clout nor the will to stamp out the problem. There is an inherent conflict of interest in an international federation's testing its own stars: Too many positive tests are not good for business in this sponsor-driven age.

Perhaps the only way to make serious inroads is for police and other conventional law-enforcement agencies to become more involved, as they did in France during the Tour.

Prince Alexandre de Merode, head of the International Olympic Committee's medical commission, reportedly said, "We will never rid sports of drugs, because cheating is part of human nature. But we can reduce it."

De Merode is correct that there will always be cheaters. It is that realization that inspires some to lobby for the use of performance-enhancing drugs to be legalized: If there is no way to stop some athletes from getting an illicit advantage, then make that advantage licit and end the inherent hypocrisy of it all. That is a seductively simple solution to a complex problem and, for me, terribly wrong-headed.

DRUG USE AT SCHOOLS

Drugs like anabolic steroids and amphetamines, and 1990's performance-enhancers of choice, erythropoietin (EPO) and human growth hormone, carry potentially significant health risks. By endorsing their use at the highest level, you exclude those competitors who wish to avoid those risks. You also endanger the health of those on the lower levels of the pyramid.

A survey by Pennsylvania State University in 1997 suggested that 2.4 percent of girls and 5 percent of boys enrolled in American high schools had used steroids.

The message that drug use is worth the risk clearly has trickled down, and condoning it at the World Cup and Grand Prix levels will only increase it in schools and clubs. But the issue is not only medical. It is also philosophical.

ADMIRING THE ARTIFICIAL

Why, after all, do sports inspire? It is not simply because athletes are powerful or graceful, or faster and more skilled than anyone before them.

It is because their performances create a connection with the spectator. There is nationalism (the French cheer for the French) and there is admiration, but how much admiration can one feel if the means to the impressive end are artificial?

It is like admiring a man with a fine toupee for his thick head of hair, or a woman who has had a facelift for her smooth skin. It is hollow, false, and one of the biggest problems with sports today is that whenever someone does something remarkable— sets a world record, runs through the pain, steps suddenly from the shadows into the light—it creates as much suspicion as it does sense of wonder.

"Shouldn't athletes, prized as models
of 'human capacity,' be allowed, nay,
encouraged, to try out drugs for the
rest of us?"

BANNING DRUGS FROM SPORTS IS POINTLESS

Robert Lipsyte

In the following viewpoint, Robert Lipsyte argues that the drug testing of athletes is unfair and that athletes should be able to use certain drugs. Lipsyte contends that sports should not be held to higher standards than the rest of society. For example, Lipsyte maintains that some therapeutic drugs such as Prozac are accepted in social use but are not permitted to be used by athletes. Furthermore, he asserts that athletes can affect the accuracy of drug tests by using masking agents and that the real issue in banning drugs concerns sports management's desire to control athletes' bodies by restricting the substances that athletes can use. Lipsyte is a writer for the *New York Times* and the author of numerous sports books, including *Idols of the Game: A Sporting History of the American Century*.

As you read, consider the following questions:

1. Why has drug testing not been fair, according to Lipsyte?
2. In the author's view, why was marathoner Alberto Salazar's use of Prozac significant?
3. According to John Hoberman, as cited by Lipsyte, why will banning testosterone in sports become impossible?

Reprinted from Robert Lipsyte, "Competition and Drugs: Just Say Yes," *The New York Times*, August 2, 1998, by permission. Copyright ©1998 by The New York Times.

A thletes have always been contemptuous of sport's attempts to regulate drug use, but they tended to keep their mouths shut. Most resented the whip hand that testing gave management, but they were too afraid of being caught, punished, or embarrassed to speak up unless they were squeaky clean, retired or busted.

ATHLETES ARE DISGUSTED WITH DRUG TESTING

Until July 1998, when bicycle racers briefly disrupted the Tour de France as a protest against what they claimed was a witch hunt, athletes have never so publicly and boldly stood up to drug testing.

One knee-jerk reaction to the slowdown in the Alps was that the inmates were taking over the asylum, another that the so-called athletes' revolt had begun again after 30 years of simmering. A day later, the race continued, probably a tribute to favors and deals. But that little mountain uprising may yet turn out to be a historical turn in the road: athletes are finally expressing justified disgust with a capricious system that seems to be, in these days of what the University of Texas professor John Hoberman calls "the therapeutic ideal," simply out of date.

If drugs like Prozac and Viagra can be taken without apology by everyday people who want to enhance their performance in a competitive world, why shouldn't athletes, prized as models of "human capacity," be allowed, nay, encouraged, to try out drugs for the rest of us?

Drug testing has not been fair—few marquee names have ever been brought down—nor as effective a deterrent as both sides would have fans believe. Athletes have gone along with the lie as long as it kept reporters from snooping around their specimens. Also, athletes have tended to stay ahead of the drug police.

A HYPOCRITICAL GAME

As the rewards for victory have spiked, a growing network of underground pharmacologists have concocted drugs too new to be detected in addition to masking agents for the old drugs. This competitive cat-and-mouse game, risky, expensive and hypocritical, has allowed athletes to continue seeking the edge while management kept the appearance of control.

That game began unraveling along with the Tour on July 29, 1998. When word reached the 140-rider pack that the police had raided a team's hotel and forcibly tested riders' urine, hair and blood for drugs, cyclists slowed down, quit, tore off their numbers, canceling the day's race.

By July 30, 1998, with a half a dozen teams out of the competition, some 101 of the 198 riders who started on July 11 in Dublin were again rolling toward Paris and $2.2 million in prizes. Apparently, the most consistent performance enhancing drug is still money.

Nevertheless, two interlocked issues, one about control and the other about appropriate drug use, were once again out of the bottle.

A Dramatic Rebellion

Not since the 1960's, when Harry Edwards, Tommie Smith and John Carlos used the Olympics as a platform against racism, Muhammad Ali used the heavyweight championship as a pulpit, and Billie Jean King led tennis players—eventually all players—out of the desert of sham amateurism, have athletes rebelled so dramatically against management.

Other labor skirmishes in 1998, including the National Basketball Association (N.B.A.) lockout, can also be seen in that context. The testing for drugs, recreational or performance enhancing (another distinction that is blurring), has always been the most subtle and insidious way of enforcing that control.

Dealing Rationally with Drugs

We may yearn for the days when cyclists only pumped up their tyres but we have to accept that those times have long gone and have been followed by the gradual departure of any substantial confidence we have in the innocence of sports in which physical effort plays the predominant part.

The first priority is to gain the ability to deal rationally with a matter that causes few tremors in everyday life. Recent developments in the impotency field, for instance, have revealed that there are some performances we don't mind being enhanced. Flippant as that may seem, drugs do occupy a more important part of our lives than they have ever done.

Peter Corrigan, *Independent on Sunday*, August 2, 1998.

And on July 27, 1998, two American Olympians—the sprinter Dennis Mitchell and the shot-put champion Randy Barnes—were suspended for possible doping offenses. Mitchell reportedly tested above the acceptable levels of testosterone.

On July 31, 1998, Barnes' B sample turned out positive, too, showing a banned nutritional supplement, androstenedione, a naturally occurring substance in the body that is available in health food stores.

A New Link Between Drugs and Sports

The most significant incident, however, may have occurred in 1994 when the marathoner Alberto Salazar ended a long streak without a victory. With the help of the antidepressant Prozac, which he was using legally as a training aid, he won the 56-mile Comrades Marathon in South Africa.

For the ever-provocative Hoberman, who wrote *Mortal Engines: The Science of Performance and the Dehumanization of Sport* in 1992, Salazar's drug of choice "forged a high-profile link between doping in sport and the wider world of pharmacology that affects us all."

Hoberman expects that "pharmacological Calvinism" will be increasingly harder to enforce in sports as drugs are "gentrified." In particular, he thinks that as more elderly men, and even women, use testosterone to enhance their lives, it will become impossible to prohibit the drug from enhancing sports performance.

The 1998 Tour ended in Paris on August 2, and the current controversy may get a flat tire; only the squeaky clean, the retired and the busted will want to talk. But the struggle for control will continue in sports, as will the hypocrisy of drug testing.

The real issue for the future will be the legalization of drugs that cross the artificial line between therapy and performance enhancement. Hoberman's vision includes Olympians at the starting blocks, "their drug company logos gleaming in the sun."

> "Beijing appears to be violating
> international norms in sports just as
> it has in ... human rights."

CHINA IGNORES ATHLETIC DRUG POLICIES

Phillip Whitten

The success of Chinese female athletes in sports such as swimming and track is suspicious and possibly the result of illegal drugs, argues Phillip Whitten in the following viewpoint. Whitten contends that record-breaking performances at the 1997 Chinese National Games are questionable because these women, many of whom were not ranked among the top fifty in their sport, are breaking longstanding records. In addition, Whitten maintains, Chinese swimmers have been more likely to test positive for steroids than athletes from any other nation. Whitten is the editor-in-chief of *Swimming World* magazine.

As you read, consider the following questions:

1. What was suspicious about the weight-lifting records set at the 1997 National Games, according to Whitten?
2. According to the author, how many Chinese swimmers have tested positive for steroids since 1991?
3. In Whitten's view, how does China's attitude toward athletic competition differ from that of the West?

Reprinted from Phillip Whitten, "Strong-Arm Tactic," *The New Republic*, November 17, 1997, by permission of *The New Republic*. Copyright ©1997, The New Republic, Inc.

W hen China's President Jiang Zemin arrived in Washington, D.C., in October 1997, he had more than just his country's growing military and economic might to crow about. At the National Games in Shanghai, Chinese athletes were busy shattering world records in everything from swimming to weight lifting. It was, by any standard, a stunning display: in the weight-lifting arena alone, Chinese women eclipsed every world record in all nine weight classes.

DISTURBING IMPROVEMENTS

But like so much of China's newfound power, there was something deeply disturbing, even frightening, about these gains. On closer inspection, the results are a little bit *too* remarkable. In some weight-lifting events, the old marks were surpassed by 60 pounds or more—in a sport which usually measures world record improvements in one- or two-pound increments. In swimming, previously unranked Chinese women set two world records, eight Asian records, and clocked the world's best time in eight of 13 individual women's events. Not since Chairman Mao Zedong reportedly swam five miles down the Yangtze River in 25 minutes have Chinese swimmers sliced so quickly through the water.

What explains this great leap forward? Dope, according to dozens of international observers. And plenty of it. "There's no question about it," said 1996 Olympic swimming champion Susan O'Neill. "The Chinese are cheating, and it's obscene." Added Australia's national swim coach Don Talbot: "It's East Germany all over again." Ironically, the latest uproar about China comes precisely at the same time investigations of more than 100 former Eastern German coaches, trainers, and physicians are beginning in Berlin. Four coaches have been charged with causing bodily harm by administering harmful anabolic steroids to minors.

China, however, seems unconcerned. After failing abysmally at the rigorously drug-tested Atlanta Olympic Games in 1996, Beijing appears to be violating international norms in sports just as it has in the areas of human rights and weapons proliferation. "Everything in my heart and my gut tells me these 'records' are fake," said assistant U.S. Olympic coach Mark Schubert, "that they've been achieved by cheating."

SUSPICIOUS SWIMMING RESULTS

Four of China's now top-ranked swimmers previously have never been among the world's top 150 in their events. Indeed, in four of the eight events in which Chinese swimmers rank first, those swimmers previously were not even in the top 50. According to Nick Thierry, secretary of the International Swimming Statisticians Association, no swimmer outside the top 50 has ever broken a world record; in Shanghai, two did.

This disparity has its own quirky logic: swimming's international governing body, Federation Internationale de Natation Amateur (FINA), only conducts unannounced drug testing on athletes listed in the top 50, leaving the relative slow pokes to use dope freely. "It saddens me every time I have to add one of these [Chinese] names to the list," said Thierry, who compiles all international records, "knowing that these performances are not legitimate."

IMPROBABLE PERFORMANCES

The times recorded by the, er, ladies in the swimming events at the China Games are incredible. They exceed the laws of probability, and therefore we should listen to the promptings of our intuitions. Training should enhance one's powers by means of the body's normal functioning. But drugs do more than just enhance normal functioning. They cause the body to behave abnormally—not unusually well but unnaturally well.

Illegal technologies are subverting the integrity of sport when we feel inclined to speak of "the body" and not "the athlete" performing well. We want sport to reward real courage, not sophisticated science. Many think this is not happening, especially when we study the times recorded in Shanghai in October 1997.

Cecil M. Colwin, Swimnews, October 1997.

Despite China's repeated denials, there are other reasons to suspect China is systematically doping its athletes in anticipation of the 2000 Olympics in Australia. The swimming records broken by Chen Yan and Wu Yanyan, for instance, had been among the toughest in the books. The 400-meter individual medley mark, by Petra Schneider, was the last remaining East German drug-aided record, but Chen lowered it by a second-and-a-half to 4:34.79, swimming some 19 seconds faster than she had in Atlanta. In the 200-meter individual medley, Wu lowered her Atlanta time by seven seconds—and chopped almost two full seconds off the world record.

Adding to the suspicions were the performances by women in the weight-lifting competition—a sport which will make its Olympic debut in 2000. Their performances "are from Mars," said U.S. Coach Lyn Jones. In fact, three lifters, including a bronze medalist, later tested positive for unspecified drugs and were disqualified. (The International Weight Lifting Federation announced it will not recognize any of the new marks.)

BREAKING TRACK RECORDS

On the track, it was much the same story, as three Chinese women destroyed the world record in the 5,000-meter run. Before the Chinese National Games, only one woman (non-Chinese) in the world had broken four minutes this year in the 1,500-meter run; in Shanghai, twelve Chinese broke the four-minute barrier.

As in 1993 and 1994, most of the Chinese distance runners are coached by the redoubtable Ma Junren of Liaoning province, who attributes his athletes' success to his special blend of turtle blood soup, caterpillar fungus, and Chinese herbs. Two years ago, Ma tried to profit from his success, peddling bottles of his concoctions for about $20 each. An independent analysis of the contents of the bottles, secured by John Leonard, chief executive of the World Swimming Coaches Association, revealed that they contained "sugar water." What may really be fueling Ma's army, experts agree, are nondetectable, genetically engineered hormones.

For Ma Junren and other coaches, there is a special incentive to use drugs at the National Games. "It's there that funds are distributed to the top coaches and athletes based on performance," noted famed Australian swim coach and anti-drugs crusader, Forbes Carlile, who coached in China during the 1980s. "A successful athlete or coach stands to earn a great deal of money by Chinese standards—many times the average annual wage."

A HISTORY OF CHEATING

If the Chinese did cheat, it would not be the first time. Since 1991, 23 Chinese swimmers have tested positive for anabolic steroids—versus just three from the rest of the world. In 1994, the Chinese responded to such revelations much as the East Germans had before them. "We do not use drugs," China's head coach Zhou Ming declared unequivocally. "Our success is due solely to hard work, innovative coaching techniques, and new technology."

One month later, as the Chinese team arrived in Hiroshima, Japan, for the Asian Games, a surprise drug test showed just how innovative those techniques were: eleven Chinese athletes tested positive, all for the same anabolic steroid—dihydrotesterone, or DHT. Because of such repeated incidents, the Chinese were banned from the 1995 Pan Pacific Championships, the first time an entire nation has been excluded from world competition for doping. None of this has apparently deterred China from trying again. Australian Mark Stockwell, a 1984 Olympic silver-medalist, advised his government that if it wants to win in 2000 it "would be better off putting eight million dollars into drug testing in China than investing it in training here in Australia."

Western democracies generally consider international sports a relatively apolitical endeavor—a way to bring nations together. But for China, as for the Soviet Union and East Germany in the past, athletics is an arena of political competition; winning demonstrates both the superiority of its political and economic system, and the greatness of its national power. "Just as our women dominate you now," Zhou Ming has said, "so will our men dominate you in four, five, six years, and so too will we dominate you in world economics." So much for constructive engagement.

"When a nation enters its athletes in competition, it accepts the reality that it must follow the rules."

THE UNITED STATES IGNORES ATHLETIC DRUG POLICIES

Asiaweek

In the following viewpoint, the editors of *Asiaweek* contend that the 1996 suspension of American swimmer Jessica Foschi, following a drug test that found steroids in her system, and the subsequent reversal of that suspension indicate that American swimming authorities operate under a double standard. *Asiaweek* argues that the U.S. Swimming Board of Review acted hypocritically when it reversed Foschi's suspension because the United States had pushed for bans of Chinese swimmers who had tested positive for drugs but backed off when it was one of their own athletes. The board's action undermines the international fight against steroid use, the magazine asserts. *Asiaweek* is an independent newsmagazine based in Hong Kong.

As you read, consider the following questions:

1. Why was Australian swimmer Samantha Riley's suspension reversed, according to *Asiaweek*?
2. According to the magazine, what was the response of the Chinese media to the decisions regarding Jessica Foschi's positive drug test?
3. Why does *Asiaweek* contend that China has successfully curbed steroid use?

Reprinted from "Double Standard: All Sport Loses If the U.S. Flouts Doping Rules," editorial, *Asiaweek*, March 22, 1996, by permission of *Asiaweek*.

Barring injuries to two of the three swimmers who finished ahead of her in an 800-meter freestyle swimming race in early 1996, 15-year-old Jessica Foschi won't be on the U.S. swim team at the Atlanta Olympic Games in July 1996. Sorry to say, it's just as well. Foschi's presence would have caused strong protests from any number of nations that didn't think she should be allowed to compete, as well as lawsuits from competitors. Foschi tested positive for steroids after a meet in 1995, but she avoided the two-year ban from competition that is the international norm.

JESSICA FOSCHI'S SUSPENSION

How come? The sad tale meanders some, but to those who recall the outrage heaped on drug-taking Chinese swimmers by foreign rivals in October 1994, it's instructive. It began when Foschi finished third at the U.S. national championships in August 1995. A subsequent drug test found in her urine traces of a male hormone used by athletes to build muscle and recover faster from workouts. In late 1995, a U.S. Swimming Board of Review slapped Foschi's wrist, essentially saying, "Don't do it again." This despite the fact that international rules mandated that she be suspended for two years. Foschi had told the review panel she had been slipped the steroids without her knowledge.

In February 1996, the Board of Directors of U.S. Swimming reversed the decision and suspended Foschi for two years as required by international swimming's governing body, known as Federation Internationale De Natation Amateur (FINA). A week later, FINA ruled that an Australian swimmer named Samantha Riley, world-record holder in two events, did not have to serve a two-year suspension for a positive drug test because the illegal drug, which was contained in a prescription headache tablet given her by her coach, did not actually enhance performance and was taken accidentally. FINA suspended the coach for two years.

Within days, U.S. Swimming reversed itself again and said Foschi would not be suspended. Board members said the FINA decision on Riley was not only a justification for them to reverse their ruling on Foschi, but made reversal imperative. Reason: U.S. Swimming would have faced—and probably lost, said the board—a court case brought by Foschi's family.

RESPONDING TO A REVERSAL

This stunning second reversal brought protests in the U.S. and abroad. Janet Evans, the only American woman to win four Olympic gold medals in swimming, put it best. "It's a big step backward," she said. "Look at the Chinese. They were banned, no questions asked about whether they were sabotaged or got the steroids from their coaches. U.S. Swimming pushed for the Chinese to be banned, but then when it happens to one of their own, they can't stand up for what they believe in. I'm ashamed."

No countries have been more critical of doping and steroid use in swimming than the U.S. and Australia—especially when it comes to China, a newly emerged power in the sport. Condemnations from those countries of Chinese swimmers reached campaign-like proportions following the Asian Games in Hiroshima in October 1994. They culminated in August 1995 in the U.S. and Australia leading a successful effort to bar Chinese swimmers from the Pan Pacific swim meet.

POSITIVE DRUG TESTS ARE IGNORED

In 1986, all members of the men's world championship team tested positive for the same banned drug in the same competition. It was the same drug pentathlon's recently hired coach had tested positive for in 1981. Over the objections of nearly every athlete at the 1986 Olympic Festival as well as U.S. Olympic Committee's (USOC's) chief medical officer, the pentathlon association and the USOC permitted all who tested positive to represent the United States. This incident gave credence to estimates of doping in pentathlon as high as 70–80 percent during the 1970s and 1980s. The U.S. Modern Pentathlon Association (USMPA) resisted efforts to control doping. Americans tested positive in the 1984 and 1988 Olympics. The USOC took no action.

In 1988–89, the USOC cut back the budget and programs of its Sports Medicine and Science Division. The USOC's chief medical officer resigned in protest. At about the same time, the USOC promoted a person to a senior executive level in USOC who admitted to authorizing and funding a blood doping program for athletes in which American athletes tested positive in international competition.

L. Richard Rader, testimony before the Senate Subcommittee on Consumer Affairs, Foreign Commerce, and Tourism, October 18, 1995.

The Chinese were notably restrained in their public responses to the February 1996 announcements. China's leading sports newspaper stated the obvious: a "double standard" was being applied. "To treat abusers of banned substances as 'making big problems smaller and small problems no problem at all' only obscures the line between right and wrong, weakens the force of deterrence and should alarm and be opposed by the international sporting world," said the *China Sports Daily*.

There's no doubt that the Chinese could speak knowledgeably on curbing the problem of steroid use. Seven of their female swimmers were suspended for two years following the Hiroshima Games. Then the Chinese successfully tackled the problem. In the first half of 1995, according to the national Olympic Committee, four of its athletes tested positive for drugs compared with 42 in all of 1994. China now has an anti-doping campaign carried out by 137 people in 23 cities.

An Issue of Integrity

At issue in the cases is not just blatant unfairness and hypocrisy, but irresponsibility. In applying different rules to its own athletes and those of other countries, U.S. Swimming undermines the international commitment to fight steroid use. On the positive side, the FINA action in the Australia case is worth emulating: suspending coaches may be a sensible alternative to penalizing youngsters who often have more ambition than sense. The core issue, though, is about integrity. The U.S. said its hand was forced by legal considerations. But when a nation enters its athletes in competition, it accepts the reality that it must follow the rules, even if that means supporting a ruling that lawyers will challenge. After all, that is the essence of competition and fair play.

| "Since athletes are role models to the rest of the student body... society has a right to regulate athletes more closely than others."

TESTING STUDENT-ATHLETES FOR DRUGS IS APPROPRIATE

Nosson Scherman

On June 26, 1995, the U.S. Supreme Court ruled that schools have the right to test student-athletes for drugs. In the following viewpoint, Nosson Scherman argues that this decision was justified. Scherman asserts that children are not necessarily entitled to the same rights as adults, in part because public safety at schools sometimes needs to take precedence over a student's individual rights. In addition, Scherman contends, student-athletes should remain drug free because they serve as role models to their peers. Scherman is the general editor of Mesorah Publications, a publisher of Jewish books.

As you read, consider the following questions:

1. In Scherman's view, why did the Supreme Court consider a drug testing case based in Vernonia, Oregon, as opposed to one set in a larger city?
2. According to the author, what was unusual about the composition of the judicial majority that decided in favor of Vernonia in the Oregon case?
3. Why does Scherman feel that student-athletes relinquish some of their rights to privacy?

Reprinted from Nosson Scherman, "Restoring a Measure of Discipline," Jewish Week, July 7, 1995, by permission of the author.

The Supreme Court handed down a ruling on June 26, 1995, that will strike embattled school teachers and administrators as a surprising return to common sense. The oldest inhabitants will remember fondly or ruefully when teachers were the law, and when children who got into trouble in school had to face the double jeopardy of irate parents, as well. That began to change more than 30 years ago when the court adopted the view that children were as entitled as adults to the constitutional guarantees of due process and the like. As the Supreme Court put it pithily in 1969, children do not "shed their constitutional guarantees at the schoolhouse gate."

As any New York City teacher will testify, that meant no more suspensions, transfers, or other meaningful punishments without documentation and hearings, even including the right to counsel. The threat of such onerous and expensive proceedings convinced principals and teachers that it was better to become selectively blind and risk aggravated neck pains from looking the other way than to attempt traditional discipline. That is the real reason why in the case of anti-Semitic letters at Norman Thomas High School [in New York City], the chancellor and the principal balked at imposing more than a slap on the wrist to offending students. The long overdue public backlash at Norman Thomas surprised everyone familiar with the school system, and though garbed in sober constitutional rhetoric, the Supreme Court decision was surely a product of the same pent-up feelings that "I'm mad as hell and I'm not going to take it any more."

RIGHTS VERSUS SAFETY

In that case, the court dealt with the tiny school district in Vernonia, Ore., a logging town with a population of only 3,000. Beset by a drug problem, the district had required random drug testing for its school athletes, even if there were no grounds to suspect an individual student. The parents of 12-year-old James Acton refused to give permission, and the district barred him from the athletic program, whereupon the parents sued.

Basing themselves on prior decisions, the lower courts found for the Actons, thus setting the stage for the Supreme Court's new front-page doctrine, which may well presage a new departure in how society deals with the constitutional dilemma of individual rights versus public safety.

The very fact that the court accepted the case indicates that it recognized the need for a re-examination of its stand that random drug testing might be an "unreasonable search and seizure," and that children had the same rights as adults. That the court chose to take such a case from a small "traditional" town, rather than from a drug-infested big city, indicates that it wanted to call attention to the universal nature of the problem.

ATHLETES HAVE LESS PRIVACY

School sports are not for the bashful. They require "suiting up" before each practice or event, and showering and changing afterwards. Public school locker rooms, the usual sites for these activities, are not notable for the privacy they afford. . . .

There is an additional respect in which school athletes have a reduced expectation of privacy. By choosing to "go out for the team," they voluntarily subject themselves to a degree of regulation even higher than that imposed on students generally. In Vernonia's public schools, they must submit to a preseason physical exam, they must acquire adequate insurance coverage or sign an insurance waiver, maintain a minimum grade point average, and comply with any "rules of conduct, dress, training hours and related matters as may be established for each sport by the head coach and athletic director with the principal's approval." Somewhat like adults who choose to participate in a "closely regulated industry," students who voluntarily participate in school athletics have reason to expect intrusions upon normal rights and privileges, including privacy.

U.S. Supreme Court, *Vernonia School Dist. 47J v. Acton*, June 26, 1995.

Sometimes the justices are so divided that they use procedural or very narrow grounds to sweep a case under the rug, even after having accepted it. A good example was another potential landmark case that was decided—or, better said, not decided—the same day as *Acton*. The issue was whether it is permissible for students, rather than clergy, to lead a prayer at graduation. Apparently the court was not ready to walk on those eggshells yet. It said that the question was moot because the students who brought the case had graduated three weeks earlier. (If only the rest of us could sidestep the tough ones as easily.)

A VARIED OPINION

In *Acton*, the court ruled 6-3 that the school board had a right to conduct urine tests. The composition of the majority in *Acton* raised eyebrows, since it included the court's most conservative members, such as Justices Antonin Scalia and Clarence Thomas, and the two Clinton appointees, Justices Stephen Breyer and Ruth Bader Ginsburg. The make-up of the majority explains some anomalies in the prevailing opinion, which reads like something of a potpourri of doctrines.

It seems obvious that Scalia, its author, had to include a variety of not necessarily consistent ideas to assemble his majority. Thus he applied a concept that has been much battered and grown rusty from disuse in recent decades: in loco parentis, i.e., that a school takes the place of parents and may therefore impose rules that would be impermissible on the part of outsiders.

Furthermore, since athletes are role models to the rest of the student body at a time when drugs are a major problem, society has a right to regulate athletes more closely than others. And since the athletic locker room, by its nature, "is not notable for its [privacy]" and "school sports are not for the bashful," an athlete implicitly relinquishes some of his right to privacy.

The last two points were undoubtedly needed to corral Breyer and Ginsburg, and they make one wonder how far the court can extend its newfound sympathy for the authority of school administrators. But if it is too early for three loud cheers, at least one or two muted ones are definitely in order. Mark Twain said, "Always try to do the right thing. Some people will be gratified and the rest will be astonished." He would have been astonished.

"No survey has ever shown that most teen-age drug users are high school athletes."

TESTING STUDENT-ATHLETES FOR DRUGS IS INAPPROPRIATE

Dave Kindred

The U.S. Supreme Court's decision in *Vernonia School Dist. 47J v. Acton*, giving schools the right to test athletes for drugs, is unfair, Dave Kindred asserts in the following viewpoint. Kindred contends that drug tests violate students' rights because students can be tested without having shown evidence of substance abuse. Kindred maintains that student-athletes submit to these tests because they lack the political power and legal backing to fight infringements of their rights. He also claims that drug use is not prevalent among student-athletes and that testing athletes is the wrong approach to addressing the larger issue of preventing drug use among young people. Kindred is a writer for the *Sporting News* and the author of several sports books.

As you read, consider the following questions:
1. What is the difficult choice public school athletes face, according to Kindred?
2. Why does Kindred believe that teenage drug users are less likely to be athletes?
3. In the author's view, what is the price of not allowing drug tests?

Reprinted from Dave Kindred, "Commentary: Drug Test Burden Unfairly Borne by Our Children," *Atlanta Journal-Constitution*, July 6, 1995, by permission of the *Atlanta Journal-Constitution*.

A ll junior high and high school athletes in America are now more than just athletes. They also are suspects. Because they are athletes and they hang with athletes, they are suspects of such notoriety that they can be compelled to prove to the authorities that they do not use illegal drugs. Which is to say they are presumed guilty until proving themselves innocent. Incredible.

AN ABSURD LEGAL SYSTEM

We're talking seventh-grade sports here, grades 7 through 12. We're talking about lining up teen-agers in order to inspect their urine for evidence of drugs. America's legal system is often absurd. Here is one more example. The Supreme Court has given public elementary and high schools permission to drug test athletes simply because they are athletes. No suspicion necessary; no probable cause necessary; no evidence of wrongdoing necessary. If you are a public-school athlete, you can be tested. By playing a game, you forfeit part of the privacy and protection against unreasonable search guaranteed by this country's Constitution.

Incredible. Has American society disintegrated so completely that to protect ourselves against our failures we now must inspect the urine of 13-year-old volleyball players? Major League Baseball is the home of Darryl Strawberry, Steve Howe and George Steinbrenner. The lords of baseball have never dared ask to drug test all athletes at all times. Nor have the National Basketball Association (NBA), National Football League (NFL) or National Hockey League (NHL) suggested it. They know better than to suggest suspension of the Constitution.

But junior high and high school athletes are children with no political power. The perpetually reprieved Howe and the given-a-felon's-second-chance Strawberry have lawyers on call. Public school athletes have no one speaking for them. So now they have a Hobson's choice. They can give up some of their rights. Or they can quit sports.

DRUG TESTING IS LUDICROUS

Such is the circumstance created by the Supreme Court's decision in an Oregon case brought by a seventh-grader who didn't want to submit to his school's drug-testing program. School district 47J in the 8,000-population logging community of Vernonia, Ore., instituted testing after a series of drug problems largely identified with athletes.

Those who support such drug testing agree with the Supreme Court's decision that the need to test outweighs the loss of privacy and protection against unreasonable search. They believe the testing is appropriate if it promotes a legitimate governmental interest, "which the prevention of drug use by children surely is," to quote columnist George Will.

Sorry. No sale here. It is ludicrous to believe that testing a few athletes—a minority at all schools—will prevent drug use by a majority of users. No survey has ever shown that most teen-age drug users are high school athletes. More likely, most users prefer a less-disciplined lifestyle that hides them from authority figures.

Hitch. Reprinted by special permission of North America Syndicate.

Common sense tells us as much. But common sense has nothing to do with the Supreme Court's decision, a 6-3 vote on the Oregon case. Instead, Justice Antonin Scalia's majority opinion says: "It seems to us self-evident that a drug problem largely fueled by the 'role model' effect of athetes' drug use, and of particular danger to athletes, is effectively addressed by making sure that athletes do not use drugs."

THE PRICE OF PRIVACY

In dissent, Justice Sandra Day O'Connor says "a mass, suspicion-less search is categorically unreasonable." Yes, she says, prohibiting such searches may allow drug users to go undetected. But she also says, "There is nothing new in the realization that

Fourth Amendment protections come with a price."

The price in this case is low. The price is missing a drug user or three. Even if we miss a thousand, better to miss them than to tell millions of innocent children—Scalia even calls them "role models"—that we think they could be guilty unless they prove to us, by handing over their urine, that they are innocent.

And once we test for cocaine and steroids, what then? Alcohol is illegal under a certain age, as is tobacco. Do we bring Breathalyzers to class? And why test only athletes? Let's test the computer wizards, the artists, the musicians, the engineers. Let's strap the teachers to a polygraph to see which of our children's custodians cheated on last year's income taxes. Yes, let's give up freedoms of privacy that men and women have died to create and sustain. Let's give them up so parents and teachers in Oregon can pass off their responsibilities to the government's drug testers.

PERIODICAL BIBLIOGRAPHY

The following articles have been selected to supplement the diverse views presented in this chapter. Addresses are provided for periodicals not indexed in the *Readers' Guide to Periodical Literature*, the *Alternative Press Index*, the *Social Sciences Index*, or the *Index to Legal Periodicals and Books*.

Michael Bamberger and Don Yaeger	"Over the Edge," *Sports Illustrated*, April 14, 1997.
Ira Berkow	"Over Fence Came Before Over Counter," *New York Times*, August 27, 1998.
Joe Chidley et al.	"Counterculture Hero," *Maclean's*, February 23, 1998.
Rae Corelli with Paul Gains	"The Drug Detectives: Technological Wizardry Will Try to Keep the Olympics Clean—but Is It Enough?" *Maclean's*, July 22, 1996.
Geoffrey Cowley and Martha Brant	"Doped to Perfection," *Newsweek*, July 22, 1996.
Jeff Galbraith	"Dazed and Confused," *Time*, February 23, 1998.
Christine Gorman	"Muscle Madness," *Time*, September 7, 1998.
Thomas Hayden and Karen Springen	"McGwire's Power Supply," *Newsweek*, September 7, 1998.
Bob Herbert	"A Hero and His Shadow," *New York Times*, August 27, 1998.
Kirk Johnson	"Performance Drugs Proliferate, and So Do Ethical Questions," *New York Times*, August 31, 1998.
New York Times	"The Olympics' Drug Problem," August 9, 1998.
Holcomb B. Noble	"Questions Surround Performance Enhancer," *New York Times*, September 8, 1998.
Skip Rozin	"Steroids and Sports: What Price Glory?" *Business Week*, October 17, 1994.
Skip Rozin et al.	"Steroids: A Spreading Peril," *Business Week*, June 19, 1995.
Mark Starr with Adam Rogers	"One More Time at Bat," *Newsweek*, July 3, 1995.

Robert Taylor   "Compensating Behavior and the Drug Testing
                       of High School Athletes," *Cato Journal*, Winter
                       1997. Available from the Cato Institute, 1000
                       Massachusetts Ave. NW, Washington, DC
                       20001-5403.

Richard L. Worsnop   "High School Sports," *CQ Researcher*, September
                       22, 1995. Available from 1414 22nd St. NW,
                       Washington, DC 20037.

FOR FURTHER DISCUSSION

CHAPTER 1

1. Several of the viewpoints in this chapter discuss the impact that parents and coaches can have on youth sports. Based on what you have read, and any relevant personal experiences, do you think that adults have a positive or negative effect on young athletes? If you feel that adults mar youth sports, what steps should be taken to improve the situation? Explain your answers.

2. Salim Muwakkil argues that the emphasis on sports in the black community sometimes leads to ostracism of students who place greater attention on academic success; William Raspberry contends that black students who seek athletic scholarships do not neglect academics because they need to maintain their eligibility. Do you think that a desire to succeed in sports aids these athletes' academic careers? Why or why not?

3. Armstrong Williams and Stephen D. Mosher write about whether athletes are, or should be, role models. Do you believe it is fair to expect athletes to be role models? Explain your reasoning.

CHAPTER 2

1. The authors in this chapter discuss various problems in college sports. Which of those problems do you think is most serious? Are there other issues in college athletics that you believe should take greater precedence? Explain your reasoning.

2. Russell Gough argues that the minimum score requirement on the SAT is unfair to many high school athletes, particularly minorities. Tom Knott contends that the minimum score is easily achievable. Should athletes be expected to achieve at least a minimum score on the SAT in order to receive a college scholarship? Why or why not?

3. Dick DeVenzio argues that student-athletes should be paid, while Gregg Easterbrook contends that these athletes should receive scholarship extensions. Which argument do you find more convincing? Why? If you think student-athletes should receive payments, what do you think would be a fair amount and why?

4. Lisa Nehus Saxon argues that the term "student-athlete" is often misused. Do you think that academics and athletics are compatible, especially at major universities? If not, what steps do you think colleges should take to ensure their athletes receive adequate educations? Explain your answers.

Chapter 3

1. The Center for the Study of Sport in Society cites a variety of statistics to support its argument that sports have yet to achieve racial equality. Which statistic, if any, do you think best supports the center's argument? Explain your reasoning.

2. Mark Whicker argues that African-American coaches who work through the system can receive promotions. The *New York Amsterdam News* contends that many qualified candidates who have relevant coaching experience are excluded from head coaching positions because of their race. Whose argument do you believe is more convincing and why?

3. Adolph Reed Jr. and Kenneth L. Shropshire differ over whether African-American athletes should speak out on racial inequality and other political issues. Do you think minority athletes should be expected to be spokespeople? Explain your answer.

Chapter 4

1. At the time her viewpoint was written, Elizabeth Arens was a college student and a member of her school's squash team. Lynette Labinger was the lawyer who represented women athletes at Brown University in a key Title IX lawsuit. Do you think their arguments are weakened or supported by their respective positions? Why or why not?

2. Steve Sailer and Stephen Seiler argue that one reason why women's athletic performances have peaked is sexism in African society. Mariah Burton Nelson contends that the performance of female American athletes will continue to improve as opportunities increase. Do you think that women's athletic talents will improve in the future? How great an impact do you think society has on women's chances of succeeding in sports? Explain your answers.

Chapter 5

1. Christopher Clarey argues that one reason why elite athletes should not use performance-enhancing drugs is because younger athletes will follow suit. Robert Lipsyte contends that athletes should be allowed to try out such drugs. Whose argument do you find more convincing and why?

2. Phillip Whitten and *Asiaweek* write about the political aspects of drug testing athletes in international competitions. Do you think that drug testing in international athletic competition has become politicized? Explain your reasoning.

3. According to Nosson Scherman, student-athletes should be role models to their peers. Do you agree with him? Why or why not?
4. Dave Kindred asserts that drug testing invades the privacy of student-athletes. He argues that such testing should be banned, even if a thousand drug users would then go undetected. Do you agree with Kindred, or do you think that the possibility of reducing drug use among teenagers outweighs his concerns over the loss of Fourth Amendment protections? Explain your answers.

Organizations to Contact

The editors have compiled the following list of organizations concerned with the issues debated in this book. The descriptions are derived from materials provided by the organizations. All have publications or information available for interested readers. The list was compiled on the date of publication of the present volume; the information provided here may change. Be aware that many organizations take several weeks or longer to respond to inquiries, so allow as much time as possible.

Canadian Interuniversity Athletic Union (CIAU)
110 Eglinton Ave. West, Suite 303, Toronto, ON M4R 1A3, CANADA
(416) 482-9933 • fax: (416) 482-8676
website: http://www.ciau.ca

CIAU is an organization designed to serve and document college sports in Canada. It offers the latest scores, scheduling, and information for the sports of all member universities as well as scholarships, athlete media coverage, and coaching assistance. The union publishes a monthly newsletter that can be read on-line and a collection of sports-related books and videos offered annually.

Center for the Study of Sport in Society
Northeastern University
360 Huntington Ave., Suite 161 CP, Boston, MA 02115
(617) 373-4025 • fax: (617) 373-4566
website: http://www.sportinsociety.org

The center's mission is to increase awareness of sport and its relation to society. It also develops programs that identify sports-related problems, offer solutions, and promote the benefits of sport. Its programs include National Student Athlete Day and the Degree Completion Program. Center publications include the annual *Racial Report Card* and an annual report.

Heritage Foundation
214 Massachusetts Ave. NE, Washington, DC 20002-4999
(800) 544-4843 • (202) 546-4400 • fax: (202) 544-6979
e-mail: pubs@heritage.org • website: http://www.heritage.org

The foundation is a public policy research institute that advocates limited government and the free market system. It opposes affirmative action for women and minorities and believes the private sector, not the government, should be relied upon to ease social problems and improve the status of women. It has numerous publications and commentaries available on sports-related subjects, with topics and titles such as subsidized stadiums and "Don't Rain on my Field of Dreams."

National Alliance for Youth Sports

2050 Vista Pkwy., West Palm Beach, FL 33411

(800) 729-2057 • (561) 684-1141 • fax: (561) 684-2546

e-mail: nays@nays.org • website: http://www.nays.org

The National Alliance for Youth Sports is a nonprofit organization that works to provide safe, fun, and positive sports for America's youth. It provides certification programs for coaches, officials, and administrators and participates in programs to prevent child abuse and encourage parental involvement in youth sports. The alliance operates the National Clearinghouse for Youth Sports Information, which provides access to many publications and instructional materials pertaining to youth sports.

National Association for Girls and Women in Sport (NAGWS)

1900 Association Dr., Reston, VA 20191

(703) 476-3450 • fax: (703) 476-9527

e-mail: nagws@aahperd.org • website: http://www.aahperd.org/nagws

NAGWS is a nonprofit organization of professional educators dedicated to achieving equality in sports for girls and women. It has produced several position papers on coaching certification, national high school championships, separate and mixed teams, and other sports-related issues concerning women.

National Association of Intercollegiate Athletics (NAIA)

6120 Yale Ave., Suite 1450, Tulsa, OK 74136

(918) 494-8828 • fax: (918) 494-8841

website: http://www.naia.org

NAIA promotes the education and development of students through intercollegiate athletic participation. Member institutions, although diverse, share a common commitment to the principle that participation in athletics serves as an integral part of the total educational process. The association features a hot line with the latest college sports information, an on-line magazine called NAIA News, and handbooks with titles such as Guide for the College-Bound Student and Guide for Students Transferring from Two-Year Institutions.

National Collegiate Athletic Association (NCAA)

6201 College Blvd., Overland Park, KS 66211-2422

(913) 339-1906

website: http://www.ncaa.org

The NCAA is the administrative body that oversees intercollegiate athletic programs. It publishes reports on student-athlete graduation rates in colleges, transcripts from its annual conventions discussing academic and athletic rules, and special reports on sports programs, finances, and television. Among its publications are NCAA: The Voice of College Sports and Guide for the College-Bound Student-Athlete.

National Strength and Conditioning Association
1955 N. Union, Colorado Springs, CO 80909
(719) 632-6722 • fax: (719) 632-6367
e-mail: nsca@usa.net • website: http://www.nsca-lift.org

The association seeks to facilitate an exchange of ideas related to strength development among its professional members. In addition to offering career certifications and educational texts and videos, the association also publishes the bimonthly journal *Strength and Conditioning*, the quarterly *Journal of Strength and Conditioning Research*, and the bimonthly newsletter *NSCA Bulletin*. Related pamphlets and resource materials include *KidsLift*, a guide to resistance training for youth, and the position paper "Strength Training and the Female Athlete."

North American Youth Sport Institute (NAYSI)
4985 Oak Garden Dr., Kernersville, NC 27284
(800) 767-4916 • (336) 784-4926 • fax: (336) 784-5546
website: http://www.NAYSI.com

NAYSI provides technical assistance to fitness centers, hospitals, sport centers, sport medicine clinics, corporations, schools, and other organizations that offer programs, products, and services for children and teenagers involving fitness, recreation, education, sport, and health. Its services are described in the *NAYSI Resource List*. It publishes a quarterly newsletter, *Sport Scene*.

Women's Sports Foundation
Eisenhower Park, East Meadow, NY 11554
(800) 227-3988 • (516) 542-4700 • fax: (516) 542-4716
e-mail: WoSport@aol.com
website: http://www.lifetimetv.com/WoSport

The foundation supports the participation of women in sports activities and seeks to educate the public about athletic opportunities for women. It publishes the quarterly newsletter *The Woman's Sports Experience*; books, including the titles *Aspire Higher—Careers in Sports for Women* and *A Woman's Guide to Coaching*; as well as an annual *College Scholarship Guide*.

BIBLIOGRAPHY OF BOOKS

Peter J. Arnold — *Sports, Ethics, and Education*. London: Cassell, 1997.

Aaron Baker and Todd Boyd, eds. — *Out of Bounds: Sports, Media, and the Politics of Identity*. Bloomington: Indiana University Press, 1997.

E. Digby Baltzell — *Sporting Gentlemen: Men's Tennis from the Age of Honor to the Cult of the Superstar*. New York: Free Press, 1995.

Jeff Benedict — *Public Heroes, Private Felons: Athletes and Crimes Against Women*. Boston: Northeastern University Press, 1997.

Susan Birrell and Cheryl L. Cole, eds. — *Women, Sport, and Culture*. Champaign, IL: Human Kinetics, 1994.

Susan Brownell — *Training the Body for China: Sports in the Moral Order of the People's Republic*. Chicago: University of Chicago Press, 1995.

Walter Byers with Charles Hammer — *Unsportsmanlike Conduct: Exploiting College Athletes*. Ann Arbor: University of Michigan Press, 1995.

Joanna Cagan and Neil DeMause — *Field of Schemes: How the Great Stadium Swindle Turns Public Money into Private Profit*. Monroe, ME: Common Courage Press, 1998.

Marcia Chambers — *The Unplayable Lie: The Untold Story of Women and Discrimination in American Golf*. New York: Pocket Books, 1995.

Pamela J. Creedon, ed. — *Women, Media, and Sport: Challenging Gender Values*. Thousand Oaks, CA: Sage Publications, 1994.

Michael N. Danielson — *Home Team: Professional Sports and the American Metropolis*. Princeton, NJ: Princeton University Press, 1997.

Laurel R. Davis — *The Swimsuit Issue and Sport: Hegemonic Masculinity in Sports Illustrated*. Albany: State University of New York Press, 1997.

D. Stanley Eitzen and George H. Sage — *Sociology of North American Sport*. Madison, WI: Brown & Benchmark, 1997.

Mary Jo Festle — *Playing Nice: Politics and Apologies in Women's Sports*. New York: Columbia University Press, 1996.

Judith E. Greenberg — *Getting into the Game: Women and Sports*. New York: Franklin Watts, 1997.

Pat Griffin — *Strong Women, Deep Closets: Lesbians and Homophobia in Sport*. Champaign, IL: Human Kinetics, 1998.

Robert S. Griffin — *Sports in the Lives of Children and Adolescents: Success on the Field and in Life*. Westport, CT: Praeger, 1998.

Allen Guttmann	*Games and Empires: Modern Sports and Cultural Imperialism.* New York: Columbia University Press, 1994.
Leslie Heywood	*Pretty Good for a Girl.* New York: Free Press, 1998.
Robert J. Higgs	*God in the Stadium: Sports and Religion in America.* Lexington: University Press of Kentucky, 1995.
John Hoberman	*Darwin's Athletes: How Sport Has Damaged Black America and Preserved the Myth of Race.* Boston: Houghton Mifflin, 1997.
Steve Hubbard	*Faith in Sports: Athletes and Their Religion on and off the Field.* New York: Doubleday, 1998.
Richard E. Lapchick, ed.	*Sport in Society: Equal Opportunity or Business as Usual?* Thousand Oaks, CA: Sage Publications, 1996.
Mike Lupica	*Mad as Hell: How Sports Got Away from the Fans—and How We Get It Back.* New York: Putnam, 1996.
Mariah Burton Nelson	*Embracing Victory: Life Lessons in Competition and Compassion.* New York: Morrow, 1998.
Mariah Burton Nelson	*The Stronger Women Get, the More Men Love Football: Sexism and the American Culture of Sports.* New York: Harcourt Brace, 1994.
Mark S. Rosentraub	*Major League Losers: The Real Cost of Sports and Who's Paying for It.* New York: BasicBooks, 1997.
Joan Ryan	*Little Girls in Pretty Boxes: The Making and Breaking of Elite Gymnasts and Figure Skaters.* New York: Doubleday, 1995.
Allen L. Sack and Ellen J. Staurowsky	*College Athletes for Hire: The Evolution and Legacy of the NCAA's Amateur Myth.* Westport, CT: Praeger, 1998.
George H. Sage	*Power and Ideology in American Sport: A Critical Perspective.* Champaign, IL: Human Kinetics, 1998.
Gary A. Sailes, ed.	*African Americans in Sport: Contemporary Themes.* New Brunswick, NJ: Transaction, 1998.
David F. Salter	*Crashing the Old Boys Network: The Tragedies and Triumphs of Girls and Women in Sports.* Westport, CT: Praeger, 1996.
Kenneth L. Shropshire	*In Black and White: Race and Sports in America.* New York: New York University Press, 1996.
U.S. House of Representatives Subcommittee on Commerce, Consumer Protection, and Competitiveness	*Stipends for Student Athletes: Hearing Before the U.S. House of Representatives Committee on Energy and Commerce, July 28, 1994.* Washington, DC: U.S. Government Printing Office, 1995.

U.S. Senate Subcommittee on Antitrust, Business Rights, and Competition	*Antitrust Issues in Relocation of Professional Sports Franchises: Hearing Before the U.S. Senate Committee on the Judiciary, November 29, 1995.* Washington, DC: U.S. Government Printing Office, 1996.
David K. Wiggins	*Glory Bound: Black Athletes in a White America.* Syracuse, NY: Syracuse University Press, 1997.
John Wilson	*Playing by the Rules: Sport, Society, and the State.* Detroit: Wayne State University Press, 1994.
Jean Zimmerman and Gil Reavill	*Raising Our Athletic Daughters: How Sports Can Build Self-Esteem and Save Girls' Lives.* New York: Doubleday, 1998.

INDEX